A Dad's Work is Never Clear

Tales of Love, Marriage, Parenting and Ice Cream. Lots of Ice Cream.

CHUCK HANSEN

ALSO BY CHUCK HANSEN

Build Your Castles in the Air: Thoreau's Inspiring Advice for Success in Business (and Life) in the 21st Century

Nose-Sucker Thingees, Weeds Whacking Back & Cats in the Bathtub: Does Life Get Any Better?

Coming soon: satirical novel and thriller
Sacrificial Lambs

Copyright © 2017 by Chuck Hansen

All rights reserved. No part of this book may be reproduced in any form or by any electronic or mechanical means, including information storage and retrieval systems, without permission in writing from the author, except by a reviewer who may quote brief passages in a review.

First Edition

The events described in these stories are loosely based on real occurrences. All characters (except for family members) have fictitious identifying characteristics and names. The author and publisher are not responsible for any third-party websites or the content of those web sites.

ISBN-13: 978-0-9973315-0-9

Ten percent of the proceeds of this book go to non-profit organizations dedicated to addressing mental health. For more information **or to get help**, contact the National Alliance on Mental Illness at www.nami.org. Or, in the Richmond, Virginia area, contact Friends 4 Recovery at www.friends4recovery.org.

Remember: it's fixable.

*For Mom and Dad.
Thank you for a beautiful example.*

CONTENTS

Foreword	i
A Groom's Work is Never Clear	1
A Bull in the China Shop	5
Hoping for a Fair Wind	8
Take my Advice: Don't Take All Parenting Advice…	12
Sink or Swim	15
Put Me In, Coach!	19
Where the Wild Woods End	23
A Girl's Best Friend	25
Pulp Nonfiction	27
Puppy Patrol	29
Teen Trauma	32
Perfect Storm	36
Valentine Validation	40
For Those Keeping Score at Home…	43
Love Doesn't Have to be a Disaster	47
The One-Sided Power of Love	51
The Fruits of Love	54
Ben and Jerry and Valentine's Month	57
The Big Ocean of Marriage	60

BOOM. It's Valentine's Day	63
Old Man, Look at Your Life	66
Dogs, Pride and Kibble	69
Yard Yarns and Fish Stories	72
Gravity, Change and the Rolling Stones	74
Slippery Slope	77
What Up, Cuz?	80
Amusement Park Musings	83
Axle-Deep in Parenting	86
You Have to Crawl Before You Can Crawl	89
My Loud, Irish, New Yorker Thanksgiving	92
Mother's Day?	95
Yes We Tan!	98
Lost in Central Park	100
Sun and Cold and Balance	102
Mid-life Catharsis	105
One Big Family	108
Dave	113
Keep Me In, Coach!	121

FOREWORD

In the foreword to my first collection of essays, *Nose-Sucker Thingees, Weeds Whacking Back & Cats in the Bathtub: Does Life Get Any Better?* (perhaps the longest / worst book title in history), I wrote that the essays in the book reflected a life that, by all rights, I do not deserve: Good friends, a one-in-a-million family, two wonderful children in Daniel and Madison, and my beautiful, funny, smart, understanding, loving wife, Stacy.

That still applies, and I thank God every day for every one of these wonderful people.

I also want to thank the publications in which some of these essays first ran for the opportunity to appear in their pages. These excellent magazines and newspapers include (in alphabetical order): the *Chesterfield Observer*, *Family Style*, *Home Style*, and *Richmond Bride*.

One additional note for the reader: since many of these essays were written several years ago, I have added "Retrospective Notes" to each essay, commenting on related changes in the world or my opinions since the initial publication. The idea was to prevent me from looking like a complete idiot in light of subsequent events, but I am pretty sure I failed.

I hope you enjoy reading this second collection of my essays, and I hope at least I've produced a better title this time. Thanks, and take care.

Chuck Hansen
Midlothian, Virginia

A GROOM'S WORK IS NEVER CLEAR
Originally published: January 2005

A word to grooms-to-be about your role in planning your wedding: if this were a football game, you would not be the quarterback. You wouldn't be the running back. And you wouldn't be the coach. On this team, you are that guy who follows the coach around on the sidelines, coiling and uncoiling the wire to his headset.

Like the wire-boy, you don't make the decisions on this team, and you would be advised against offering opinions about decisions to the leaders of this team. Your job – your only job – is to keep up, be ready for direction changes, support the coach no matter what happens, and otherwise be invisible unless called upon directly.

The fact of the matter is that, during the wedding planning, the guy gets one decision. So choose that decision carefully.

In my case, my decision was to invite all of my 25 aunts and uncles, my 60+ first cousins and their spouses and kids. My wife's family, which counts no aunts, no uncles and no first cousins, never had a chance. They planned (and, significantly, paid for) a wedding that was out of control the minute the church doors opened.

So, I got a break on my decision. But that doesn't change the underlying fact for guys: your wedding is not about you. Your bride (and likely her mom) has been planning this event since childhood. Before your fiancé knew what she wanted to be when she grew up, she knew she wanted to be a beautiful bride in a beautiful wedding.

Now, just because that statement is offensive doesn't mean it's not true. Here's another one: the man is entirely incidental to a wedding. *The flower guy* is indispensable. The groom, on the other hand, is a plug-and-play, a bolt-on. If he weren't there, it would be some other guy, and not a thing would be different.

What makes this difficult is the fact that guys are problem-solvers, as we all learned reading *Men Are from Mars; Women Are from Venus* while sitting in the bathroom. For most guys, being engaged-but-unempowered is like Hell Week in college, except it's 52 times longer.

Like it or not, though, it's the right call. I mean, you're a *guy*. Think about how the wedding would turn out if you were in charge:

- Planning would begin one week before the ceremony.
- Invitations would be black-and-white photocopied flyers, folded twice, stapled and mailed.
- Flowers? Get real.
- All the wedding pictures would be self-taken from arm's length.
- Caterers? One word: Domino's.
- Funnel hits at the bar.
- The first dance would be a toss-up between *Smoke on the Water* and *Why Don't We Get Drunk* ...

The only potential improvement we might make: the bridesmaids' dresses. Forget purple taffeta or an off-brown silk tarp. If it were up to the guy, the bridesmaids would have dresses that made them look HOT. This, of course, would be for the benefit of the groomsmen.

Once the guy gets over his natural tendency to want to take charge, he finds that it's good *not* to be the king, because there are scores of no-win decisions.

For example, finding a church that is available on the month and day that you want to get married is easy… if you don't care what year you get married. In the unlikely event you actually do find an available church in the near future, it's probably a random house of worship that you lucked into. The problems with this:

- The church is tucked into a suburb of town that you didn't know existed, 35 miles from the only reception hall that has availability that same weekend.
- The minister is an unknown quantity. True stories: during one wedding I attended, the minister sprung a surprise sermon asserting that most of the attendees will burn in Hell. Before another wedding, we were greeted in the parking lot by a cigar-smoking preacher with a drink in one hand and the other hand casually tucked halfway into the back of his pants. That guy's sermon ended up going in more circles than a NASCAR race.
- As you might expect, the ministers at other churches usually take their calling seriously. The result: mandatory pre-wedding "classes" for the couple that teach the traditions of a religion that, up until now, you thought only existed in the old Eastern Block.
- Then there is the "sex talk" with the minister, which manages to be even more awkward and uncomfortable than the one you had with your dad when you were ten, mainly because this time your fiancé is a part of the discussion.

So, wire-boy, all this is to say that when it comes to planning weddings, it's great to be the guy.

Retrospective Notes for *A Groom's Work is Never Clear*

- This essay, published in January 2005 in the glossy *Richmond Bride* magazine, was therefore written around September 2004, which feels like not long after the Cuban Missile Crisis.
- Which explains some amazing differences between life then and now, such as the concept of a wire-boy (headsets are all wireless now), paper flyer invites (I'm guessing texts would be the mode of communications now… or Twitters? Or SnapVines? Whatever.), and *that* Jimmy Buffett anthem which has faded into the mists of history.
- However, I *would* like some credit for the first published reference to "selfies," which I called "photos self-taken at arm's length." I will grant that "selfies" is much pithier.
- Other than that, the rest of the details in this essay are still valid, including our marriage, I'm happy to say. ☺

A BULL IN THE CHINA SHOP
Originally published: July 2005

We've all heard what happens when a bull gets in the china shop, but no one ever asks the obvious question: why did they let him in there to begin with?

I know the answer: the bull asked a china doll to marry him, and she said yes. Then they *had* to let him in.

My family immigrated to Virginia from Brooklyn early in 1965, the first Yankees on our block since Grant came through on his way to Appomattox, a hundred years earlier almost to the day. Both my parents were from big families, with 17 siblings between them, and they brought south three kids separated by just 25 months (a.k.a., Irish triplets) (and another baby coming soon) and a family culture that was boisterous, outgoing and almost compulsively communicative.

Stacy's family is nearly exactly opposite. Quiet, dignified and proper, they are Virginia natives from many generations back, with two kids and zero aunts and uncles. Conversations are polite, demeanors are reserved and there isn't a room in their house that couldn't go straight into the next *Southern Living*.

Now, a key challenge in any marriage is managing the entry of a new person into each side's family culture, and it's usually hardest on the more reserved family. In our case, there was no doubt which family would bear the brunt of the culture clash.

I came into Stacy's family like Rodney Dangerfield entering Bushwood Country Club, like Godzilla sauntering into Tokyo. There may have been shock and consternation all around me, but I didn't notice – I was too busy using the wrong fork, double-dipping in the Ranch dressing and knocking delicate figurines off low tables with my trademark Hansen Bubble Butt. (The upside: by the time we had kids, Stacy's parents' house was child-proofed because they had been forced to relocate all their breakable stuff above butt level.)

By far, Stacy had the harder assignment in adjusting to my family. I remember an early meal at my parents' house where this became glaringly clear.

First of all, mealtime at our families' respective homes are vastly different experiences. In Stacy's family, no one starts eating until everyone is seated and has their food, cloth napkins rest in laps, entrées are always accompanied by a half-dozen side dishes, condiments sit in little dishes on the table, dinner conversation is polite and carried on using "inside voices," and everyone has a regular, if not assigned, seat.

No matter how many times a guest says "I'm so full I'm going to explode," he can count on being offered more of each dish several times before he finally rolls himself away from the table.

All of this is wonderful, of course, and even though it was not my normal family dining environment (in which I am most comfortable), I was able to adjust easily, because it was simply a matter of dialing back my... let's call it exuberance (a personality trait that is the combined result of nature, nurture and choice).

Stacy, reserved and demur, faced a drastically more difficult challenge in dealing with my family's mealtime traditions, as became clear one evening during our courtship.

The meal was cold-cut sandwiches, laid out buffet style on the counter. My family fell on the spread like sharks on a bleeding surfer. Stacy stood politely aside, allowing others to serve themselves first. As we got our food, each of us scrambled for a seat on the far side of the table (where you are less likely to be asked to go get stuff from the kitchen). The din and chaos rose steadily as conversation was joined and friendly disagreement immediately established, various items were found missing (*Hey, get me the milk, will ya'?* and *I don't have a napkin!* and *Here, use these paper towels!*), and stories – some decades old and *still* developing – were exchanged.

Meanwhile, Stacy remained at the end of the buffet "line," confident the meal wouldn't start until all were seated.

Needless to say, Stacy was more than a little surprised when, just as she sat down in the one remaining chair, my dad pushed back from a loud debate about religion *and* politics *and* abortion and said, "Well, *that* was good! What's for dessert?"

Stacy adjusted admirably that day, but I don't think she's ever gotten completely comfortable with this culinary equivalent to the running of the bulls. I, on the other hand, am perfectly content with my role in her family's china shop. It's good to be the bull.

Retrospective Notes for *A Bull in the China Shop*
- It is only now, more than a decade after I wrote this second essay in the space of six months for *Richmond Bride* magazine (the first was *A Groom's Work is Never Clear*, above), that I realize that the last sentence in both essays are almost identical. Oopsy?
- For the Dated Reference file: Rodney and Bushwood.
- Stacy is still a little uncomfortable.

HOPING FOR A FAIR WIND
Originally published: February 2003

"God, grant me the serenity to accept the things I cannot change, the courage to change the things I can, and the wisdom to know the difference."
— Reinhold Niebuhr (The Serenity Prayer)

Interesting fact about sailboats: They need wind to sail. Interesting – and also related – fact about the wind: It doesn't always blow. Put those interesting facts together and you are adrift on the ocean.

Imagine the calmest pond you have ever seen, without the slightest breeze to disturb the absolutely unrippled surface. So quiet you could see a pin drop in the water. It's called "the doldrums." When I was 25, I spent three straight days in the doldrums, in the middle of the Bermuda Triangle, during an Atlantic crossing I made in a 51-foot sailboat named *Jaska*.

During our time in the doldrums, the motionless Atlantic mirrored the sky and clouds above so perfectly that it was impossible to tell where the blue-and-white canopy above ended and the ocean, reflecting that canopy, began. Water and sky melted together, creating the illusion of a horizon just a dozen yards off our rail.

The effect was disturbing. Rather than sailing astride the vast, tossing waters of the Atlantic, it felt as if we were floating motionless in the dead air of a small crystal globe.

The halyard slapped against the mast with a metallic ring as *Jaska* bobbed slightly on the becalmed sea. Beyond this sound, the silence was thunderous. Not a wave broke, not a fish jumped, not a line creaked as it strained to hold our sails against the wind.

Ian, our extraordinarily competent first mate from Antigua, even tried whistling for the wind, an old sailors' trick, and still we were stuck. We ran the engine from time to time to make a little progress. But we didn't have enough fuel to motor across the ocean. The wind would be our only ride out of here.

My three crew mates, experienced sailors all, were not worried.

I, however, was worried. In fact, at first I was reasonably sure that our being literally adrift in the Atlantic constituted some sort of emergency. It didn't.

We weren't out of water or food; we weren't suffering from exposure; we weren't injured. We were just stuck. It was a vividly tangible lesson that sometimes you have a significant lack of control over your own forward progress.

All you can do in such a situation is affect that which is within your control. So we did. We made the best of it. We cleaned the boat and performed maintenance and read and got to know each other better.

(One of the crew was my good friend Dave, whom I'd met in the Virgin Islands, and who'd insanely suggested I take part in this journey. I'd met the captain, Dimitri, and first mate, Ian, about three weeks earlier, just two weeks before we set sail.)

Eventually the wind returned, as it always does. And not only were we ready for its return, but I was now better prepared for the inevitable next time.

Ten years later, almost to the day, I sat next to my newborn daughter, Madison Claire, as she slept peacefully. We were not, however, in a peaceful place. We were in the pediatric intensive care unit of a hospital.

Barely a week into her life, Madison was struck by Respiratory Syncytial Virus (RSV), a dangerous virus that can kill a little one like her.

During the first few days of Madison's illness, my wife, Stacy, and I, and our families were tossed in the waves of a storm we never saw coming. Madison's condition deteriorated from bad to worse as her lungs foundered and began taking on fluid and mucus too rapidly. We realized that we could lose our precious little girl.

But through God's will and our doctors' and nurses' skill – and Madison's fighting spirit – she was brought out of immediate danger after a few days in the storm.

Then, in the early morning hours of day five in intensive care, we were becalmed. The medical staff had worked to stabilize Madison, to put her in a position from which she could recover. But only Madison and God could provide the healing wind that would deliver her and us from this sterile hospital room, back to the lovingly prepared nursery that waited at home.

So we waited – watching CNN, sleeping on uncomfortable recliner chairs by the bed, fielding calls from relatives and eating fast food and hospital grub. And we held our little girl every minute that she was awake.

On the morning of day six, I went down to the gift shop to buy a treat for my wife, to try to help cheer her up some. Behind the register, on a plaque on the wall, I saw the Serenity Prayer, and I thought immediately back to those becalmed days on *Jaska*. I spent a moment swimming in this reflection.

Then I said a prayer for my daughter, bought some candy for my wife, and whistled as I walked back to the intensive care unit, hoping for a fair wind soon.

Retrospective Notes for *Hoping for a Fair Wind*
- Two days later, Madison was released from the hospital, after a quicker-than-expected recovery.
- This year, our healthy, beautiful little girl turned 19 years old. Madison will be a sophomore in college next fall. She is an amazingly talented artist, and a smart, funny and kind person.
- In a sad postscript, however, my friend Dave passed away suddenly while I was editing this book. I have added an essay about Dave and what he meant to me toward the end of this book. I will miss him very much.

TAKE MY ADVICE: DON'T TAKE ALL PARENTING ADVICE...
Originally published: October 2009

This just in from the newly created federal "You're Not a Failure as a Parent Department" (YNaFaaPD): A six-month-old baby often behaves more like a pooping, screaming potted plant than a bundle of joy.

And screaming, pooping potted plants don't provide very satisfactory adult interaction – which your adult mind must have. Therefore, if you are a stay-at-home mom or dad, and you find yourself experiencing long stretches of mind-numbing boredom, it's not because you are a bad parent. It's because you are normal. So don't feel guilty (easier said than done).

Just wait until the kid gets old enough for videos. The stuff that makes toddlers laugh makes adults want to knock themselves unconscious with Tonka® toys.

Another bulletin: Unhappiness in life is often caused when what you expect doesn't match reality. And a lot of our initial child-rearing expectations are foisted on us by others. (By the time you get to the second child, you know the deal and don't listen to all those people.)

For example: making baby food yourself instead of buying it in the jars (which must be OK for babies because they clearly are marked with a picture of a healthy baby on the label). I know the *What to Expect...* book series is the unquestioned source of all baby-raising wisdom, but when I got to the part where they wanted us to "mash" our own baby food, I nearly went back to getting my advice from Jon and Kate.

Then there's the baby-naming conundrum. Stacy and I have wonderful parents and relatives and felt no pressure to name our children after family members, Civil War generals, favorite football teams, etc. However, just to be sure, we didn't tell anyone our kids' names until the ink was dry on the birth certificates. That way we also avoided putting people in the tough spot of pretending to like the names we were planning to bestow on our kids.

Of course, who could possibly not like the names we chose: "Madison Ardwinna Stonewall Redskins Hansen" and "Daniel Leif Ericson Paddy O'Guthrie Hansen"?

We even had a pediatrician at one point who didn't want us to use those nose-ball sucker-thingies to clear the baby's nose. Instead, he wanted us to take a syringe of saline, shoot it up one nostril (of the baby) and all the gunk would come pouring out the other nostril. Well, I am not going to just throw away one of the most effective medical tools ever devised by Western, Eastern and Northern / Southern medicine (if there ever was such a thing). (Feel free to write in now to defend Northern / Southern medicine although, let's face it, surgical instruments during the Civil War consisted either of a hacksaw or a pistol.) (But I digress.) (You think??)

In reality, there are very few parents out there who should feel guilty about the job they're doing. (Insert another Jon and Kate joke here.)

Just do your best, correct your mistakes when you make them, take good advice and disregard bad advice guilt-free, and love your kids.

And it's always best to keep those baby names to yourself until it's too late. Just ask young Madison Ardwinna Stonewall Redskins and Daniel Leif Ericson Paddy O'Guthrie.

Retrospective Notes for *Take My Advice: Don't Take All Parenting Advice...*

- Wow, I was right about Jon and Kate. A regular Nostradamus.
- My editor cut the digression about Civil War medicine. I put it back because I can. I'm sure she was right though... ☺
- She also cut a line about Paris Hilton, which she was ABSOLUTELY right about.
- The bit about giving Madison "Redskins" or "Stonewall" as a middle name has morphed into an entirely different joke since 2009.

SINK OR SWIM
Originally published: November 2005

If your kids ever ask for a fish, keep in mind these words from Ecclesiastes and the Byrds: "To everything there is a season ... a time to mourn and a time to dance."

Unless you have fish. Then *every* season is a time to mourn.

Our 9-year-old son, Daniel, recently got some pet fish, and at first things went swimmingly. But after a while, the aquarium water had gotten so dirty that the fish left little clearish trails behind when they swam. It was time for a water transfusion.

The very first step was to get the fish – Polka-Dot and Golden, two pale-orange cloud fish less than an inch long – safely out of the tank. And that's when the operation went completely south.

I'd just gotten the fish into little bowls when Stacy walked in and immediately began screaming and pointing. "The ... FISH!" she shrieked. "The FISH!" she repeated, and then finally, "On ... on ... ON the FLOOR!"

I looked, and sure enough, there was Polka-Dot (or Golden) lying on the floor, after apparently leaping for his freedom toward the neighborhood lake and falling short by just 600 feet. Stacy picked the little orange fish off the linoleum and dropped him into the bowl, and we watched for hints of injury. The first hint came when the fish floated to the surface like a kid's helium balloon to the ceiling.

Just then Daniel's quavering voice reached up the stairs: "Are … my fish OK?"

My policy is to be truthful with my children whenever possible. "Well, actually…," I began.

Daniel's instant, sorrowful wail drowned out the rest of my words. I didn't need to hear, though, to understand Stacy's opinion of my answer.

Meanwhile, Polka-Dot (or Golden) was bobbing around his bowl with his tongue out and those little Xs over his eyes.

"*Go get another fish!*" Stacy commanded, in a whispered yell so sharp it nearly left a mark. I reluctantly agreed. But in the meantime, I told her, she would need to keep Golden (or Polka-Dot) moving forward so water could flow through his gills, getting oxygen to his brain.

And she thinks watching fishing shows is a waste of time.

I left her with the tiny fish between two fingers, pushing him around the bowl like a little toy boat in the bathtub.

As I grabbed my keys and wallet and headed for the door, Daniel turned, teary-eyed, and asked where I was going. "To get more rocks for the aquarium," I fibbed.

Daniel's a smart kid. At that point, he could only have concluded that his dad is either a liar or an idiot with no ability to prioritize during crises.

When I got to the pet store I ran to the fish section and finally found an unkempt teenage employee.

"I need an orange cloud fish!" I said breathlessly.

"An orange fish?" the kid repeated, slowly.

An orange cloud fish!"

"We've got lots of cloud fish."

"Do you have orange cloud fish?"

"We've got orange goldfish."

"I need an orange *cloud fish!*"

"We've got lots of cloud fish."

"*Are any of them orange?!*"

"The goldfish are orange."

"TAKE ME TO THE CLOUD FISH!"

Unfortunately, he was right. They had orange fish and they had cloud fish, but they had no orange cloud fish. So I grabbed a bagful of aquarium rocks and headed home, defeated.

I found Stacy leaning over the bowl where I'd left her performing fish CPR 45 minutes earlier. There, in the bowl, was the tiny orange cloud fish, swimming clumsily around. Every time he stopped swimming, he would roll over and float to the surface, and then his tail would kick in and he'd stumble around some more.

"I think he might make it," Stacy whispered.

By the next morning, Polka-Dot (or Golden) was back in his tank, swimming like a drunken sailor, banging into colorful boat wrecks but no longer floating heavenward. He'd made it, that little fish, albeit with some apparent brain damage (to the extent that a brain with only two seconds' worth of memory could be damaged).

Since then Daniel's fish tank has continued to provide circle-of-life lessons. And as painful as they are, I've come to understand their value. Still, I think if we ever decide to get another pet, I'll be leaning toward something a little more durable. Like a giant tortoise, maybe. Or a redwood tree.

Retrospective Notes for *Sink or Swim*
- A couple years later, not having learned our lesson, we got our daughter Madison a fish. And, sure enough, I walked into her room one day and that damn fish was floating on the top of the water, dead. So I called Madison in, and I broke the news to her as gently as I could: her fish had died. Madison burst out crying, inconsolable, and I pulled her close in a hug. Her heart was broken. As she sobbed into my shirt, I looked over at the aquarium and… that… DAMN FISH… was swimming again.

- I will say it again: never, never, never, never get your kid a fish. Never.

PUT ME IN, COACH!
Originally published: Spring 2003

April is easily the cruelest month of the year. No one has any illusions about February. March flat out bills itself as either coming in or going out like a lion, so no surprises there. And, of course, May is a shoe-in for good weather – by then there are so many new flowers that the world smells like one big funeral home.

No, April is the heartbreaker. Spring is officially nearly two weeks old by the time April Fools' Day initiates this pitiless month.

The reason for the April letdown is simple: our childish expectations of warmer days are dashed time and again by a weather pattern of brief spells of frigid sunshine sandwiched between squall lines of cold rain.

But no matter the weather, there is one April arrival that you can always count on: baseball.

Not professional baseball. I've got as much interest in professional baseball these days as I do in which professional preacher is coming out with a new book.

No, I'm talking about youth baseball. Specifically, peewee baseball.

My son plays. He'll be seven this year.

For the past two years, I've coached. Yessir. Coached peewee baseball. They say coaching peewee baseball is like herding chickens. That's true, except you never have to try to convince ten chickens to stand in one place in a field for 30 minutes.

In truth, coaching peewee baseball is probably closer to leading the Hyperactive Chicken Precision Marching Troupe.

The joys and the challenges of coaching peewee baseball, of course, come from the peewees playing it. Coaching kids this young is a series of interesting psychological experiments. You never know what they'll latch on to.

For example, I remember a kid early in the season who let a bad pitch go by him once. I told the kid he had a "good eye!" for not swinging at the errant pitch. From then on, the kid watched every ball go by and wouldn't have swung if they had pitched him a beach ball underhand. He may not have known how to hit very well, but he *knew* that he knew how to watch a ball go by and by God he was going to go with his strength.

Then there are the distractions. Professional athletes have to deal with distractions such as contract negotiations, concealing performance enhancing drug use, gun laws, etc. A six-year-old athlete has distractions too. Like planes. And kites. And birds. And the game being played over on the other field. And whatever that is up his nose. And, the most devastating, most vexatious distraction of them all: dirt.

It's weird. It's primal. Kids on a baseball field are compelled to play in dirt like dogs are compelled to roll in poop.

Using his foot, or squatting down to dirt level, the peewee baseball player will draw lines in the dirt. He'll draw circles. He'll draw squares in circles with a line through them. He'll pick up a handful of dirt and pour it slowly into the other hand, like a farmer sifting his soil before planting season. He'll throw dirt into the air. He'll throw dirt at the other team's third base coach. He'll pour the dirt into his hat, then put his hat on his head, and look around with an expression on his face like, "Now *that's* a good use of dirt!"

Then, when I say, "What are you doing?" he'll look at me like it was the dumbest question since Flounder asked the guys if they were playing cards.

But there's another side. Once, early in my first season of coaching, one of our kids hit a nice shot over second base and into the outfield. He ran to first base jumping up and down like he'd just won the World Series with a walk-off homer.

I ran over to tell him what a good job he did. When I reached him, I knelt down and put up my hand so he could give me a high-five – and the kid jumped off the bag and caught me with a surprise hug. The perfect joy in that kid's eyes was unforgettable, and it reminded me immediately of my first hit, playing in the Bethlehem Little League off Lakeside Road some 35 years before.

It had sneaked up me. It still does. On a bright Saturday morning in April, when you're kneeling in the dirt trying to get a kid to square up with home plate when he bats, or out in the field showing him how to stay down on a ground ball – it will sneak up on you.

A whiff of a leather baseball glove. The feel of a bat in your hands. The smell of fresh cut grass and the sound of a sideline full of cheering parents in lawn chairs and on blankets. The sun shining off the faces of players who don't know how to grandstand... who wouldn't charge for an autograph even if they could write their name in cursive... who play for the joy and the excitement and the hope that today they might be the one to hit the home run and circle the bases (maybe even in the right direction), and get that game ball.

It sneaks up on you. It all comes back.

It is rebirth in April, through the eyes of a peewee baseball player.

Retrospective Notes for *Put Me In, Coach!*
- When I was reviewing this essay for the book, I almost revised the part about having as much interest in professional baseball as I do in professional preachers. It felt like a pretty negative statement about professional

baseball, but then I remembered that, in 2003, the revelations were beginning to come out about pro ball players using performance-enhancing drugs. The amazing thing about the whole steroids-in-baseball issue was that we were surprised. Imagine the national suspension of disbelief necessary to accept that these players were *suddenly* smashing home run records all on their own. Even as these former mortals transformed into muscle-bound cartoon characters the size of Macy's Thanksgiving Day Parade balloons, we were discussing the possibility that the *baseballs* were juiced.

- My comparison of baseball players to preachers is apt. Televangelism is another world where people we want to admire have consistently fallen short of our expectations.
- But is it ever good to invest ourselves in the behavior of public figures? Great men and women often – always, probably – have feet of clay. They are admirable but flawed, and inevitably they disappoint.
- It is better to invest yourself in the great *ideas* that are *embodied* by great people, like the Constitution or the Golden Rule or civil disobedience or baseball as a game rather than as big business.
- And better yet to invest yourself in that which you can at least partially control, like the experience you help create on a pee wee baseball diamond, or just the appreciation of a world waking up from winter to another glorious spring.

WHERE THE WILD WOODS END
Originally published: October 2004

My kids bring home a lot of homework dealing with The Environment, and as I watch them labor it occurs to me that the environment has changed a lot in the 35 or so years since I was their age. I don't mean more polluted or less, although it's definitely one or the other. I mean the environments that each respective generation lived in or lives in are very different from each other.

When I was a kid, The Woods were down at the end of our short street, a wild, overgrown swath of hardwoods split by a sliver of water we called The Creek. This stand was our daily playground. Beyond The Woods were grassy fields and dilapidated chicken coops, and the weathered old cinder-block house where The Farmer with the Shotgun lived.

For my kids, the woods are neatly corralled in a county park five miles and a 20-minute drive away, veined by jogging trails and augmented with modern playground equipment anchored in 18 inches of impact-softening mulch chips.

As kids, we experienced summer showers sitting in the street gutter in front of our house, channeling the storm water runoff with our bodies and building dams out of driveway gravel and sticks.

Nowadays, the closest my kids get to rushing rainwater is watching it pour over the clogged gutters hanging off the front of our house. After all, the radar shows a thunderstorm 17 miles west, and that's nearly close enough to take a child whose parents are foolish enough to let him out of the house.

As kids, we wasted hours catching lightning bugs, honey bees and June bugs in jars, poking sticks into crawdad holes down by The Creek, running barefoot across cool grass on warm evenings, and going fishing – just us kids – at the small lake tucked into a corner of our neighborhood.

Now kids spend their "free" time running the grass of soccer and baseball fields, have never even seen a June bug (what happened to those, anyway?), couldn't tell a crawdad hole from a pile of dirt, and fish twice a year, always under the close supervision of hyper-careful parents like me.

Institutionalized environmental education in grade schools has done much to raise awareness about the perils we present to our planet. But there is no substitute for kids getting their hands dirty, literally. All they need from us is the time and, mostly, the permission.

Retrospective Notes for *Where the Wild Woods End*
- No change, unfortunately.

A GIRL'S BEST FRIEND
Originally published: August 2009

I can't say that I blame her, really (jeez, if I had a dollar for every time I've had to say *those* words…).

My toddler daughter Madison and I were in the yard when a neighbor's Golden Retriever bounded over to say hello. This was a big, beautiful dog – well, that was my perspective. To Madison, the dog was enormous and terrifying.

If you've ever seen a cat go up a tree ahead of a pursuing canine, you have some idea of how Madison ended up on my shoulders at that moment, shrieking and screaming all the way up. For the dog (and the neighbor, by the way), this was a non-event and life went on. For Madison (and our family), this was a life-changing moment, because she was now very afraid of dogs. All dogs.

That meant the universe of places we could go and friends we could visit shrank dramatically. If there was a dog, or even the remote possibility of a dog, then either we weren't going or we were leaving Madison at home (and there are rules about that). The phobia was so engrained I was sure Madison would have it for life.

A little fear can be good, particularly with dogs. But a lot of fear, about anything, is debilitating. Fear can define and limit us – what we are willing to try and what think we can become.

Then, last October, we found ourselves in the cool shadow of Old Rag Mountain on a farm looking at a litter of Labradoodle puppies. Ten-year-old Madison had consented to consider a puppy, and the Labradoodle was one of several breeds we'd identified as the right size and, more importantly, the right temperament.

Of the five black fur balls rolling around the small pen, a couple were bruisers, a couple were middleweights, and one was a small slip of a pup, timid but friendly. After a few moments of trepidation, we were in the car and headed back to Midlothian, the shy, dark puppy snuggled up to Madison in the back seat. We named her "Bailey."

There were nips and bites along the way and sometimes I thought Madison might slide back into her canine-phobia. But she hung in there – I think she loves Bailey so much that she'd resolved to keep trying.

While I bought five dog-training books and read two chapters in one of them, Madison took it upon herself to train Bailey to sit, lie down and shake.

This summer, Madison and her friend Peyton started a business: Walk 'n Watch ("We walk your dog, we watch your dog, we do both!"). The girls are considering volunteering at the SPCA and have decided they will be dog breeders together when they grow up.

The magnitude of the change in Madison has been breathtaking. A book I'm reading, *Taming your Gremlin* by Rick Carlson, has taught me a lot about dealing with and defeating the gremlin of fear that sabotages dreams and aspirations. But even more inspirational and motivating has been seeing my daughter (with help from girl's best friend) overcome her fears and take so large a step toward a fuller and more fulfilling life.

Retrospective Notes for *A Girl's Best Friend*
- Madison and Bailey are still BFFs.

PULP NONFICTION
Originally published: April 2010

Our annual allotment of 12 yards of mulch was delivered over the weekend, and I have spent the last several days pitching and spreading.

I used to look forward to this test of endurance – me against the pile (that's not a metaphor – I mean the pile of mulch) in a one-day race to sundown.

Over the years, my lofty goals have devolved – place all the mulch by the end of the weekend, then the week, then the month, then the end of spring, and now I'm happy if I'm not brushing snow off the pile as I finish the job.

So, naturally, this column was going to be about the impact of middle age on my speed-mulching career.

Then I realized this column would run on April 7, my mom's 70th birthday.

I know you were looking forward to hearing about back pain and *plantar fasciitis* and the challenges of keeping ear hair in check, but I'm going to write about my mom instead.

Mom was born in 1940, eighth of 12 kids (how about those Irish Catholics?), at the tail end of the Depression. I've written before about how the Depression-era sensibilities Mom tried to teach us have come in handy during the past couple of years.

But, as Dad might say, economic downturns come and go, but family never seems to leave no matter how obvious your hints. The lessons Mom taught us about family are permanent and always applicable, while the recipe for dirt soup is something you want to break out only when necessary.

With 12 kids in Mom's family, a sort of tribal mentality came into play, where the parents raised the oldest children and the oldest raised the youngest and the youngest always knew there were 13 people who absolutely had their back.

And Mom instilled the same ethic in her children: We always knew our siblings had our back. We might have fought like the Hatfield cats and McCoy dogs, but when push came to shove (and it sometimes did), I knew Kathy, Linda and Ken were with me, and they still are.

Mom also drilled home the importance of honesty in the family. Once, while my parents were out, a male sibling put his foot through a wall in anger (I'm not saying who, but it was Kenny). When Mom got back, he tried to tell her that he'd jokingly tossed an orange at the wall and accidently created the hole.

Mom, knowing she'd been lied to, stomped to the kitchen and reappeared seconds later with a huge navel orange, which she then flung at the wall as hard as she could. Instead of piercing the wall, the orange exploded on impact, showering the room with pulp and dramatically disproving Kenny's – ahem, I mean the boy's – alibi.

The lesson stuck (as did the orange juice), and to this day we do not lie to each other, and we do not keep navel oranges in our homes.

So, for a lifetime of lessons and laughs and memories, I want to thank you, Mom. Happy birthday, and I love you!

P.S. Beat that, Ken.

Retrospective Notes for *Pulp Nonfiction*
- Hahahahahahahahaha, Kenny…

PUPPY PATROL
Originally published: April 2009

Our dog is now 7 months old, which means she still has the explosive, inexhaustible energy of a puppy, but now she also has the long legs, stride and speed of a big dog.

This isn't a problem in the house – it's a closed circuit, the wood floors are slick as ice, and we can corral her when necessary. But when the door opens, it is absolutely critical that I catch her at the doorstep or, as a last resort, on the porch, because once she gets into the open yard, she ain't coming back until she's good and ready.

Unfortunately, a 7-month-old puppy versus a man 79 times her age (people years) is not nearly an even match. I flail and reach and lunge and dive, usually pulling several muscles and grabbing air, like Wile E. Coyote after the Road Runner.

Then she's on her turf, bounding out of reach across the greening grass and mocking her obedience training. What's worse, she's fool enough at this age to follow a squirrel out into the street and into the path of a car.

As we all learned in high school biology, automobiles are the evolutionary response to squirrel overpopulation. But dogs can easily fall victim to speeding cars, too.

If you think about it, kids (especially teenagers) are just puppies with better smelling breath. If we want to keep our kids out of trouble, then, like puppies, it's much better to catch them on the porch than to try to rein 'em back in once they're out in the open. Because once they're out there, we can't be everywhere. We can't watch them every minute.

But it used to be that parents didn't have to be everywhere, because everyone else in the neighborhood was watching the kids, too. Parents were neighborhood watch before Neighborhood Watch was cool. It was a social contract. You were obligated as a parent to keep an eye on other parents' kids, and to report back if something fishy was going on.

Sure, some parents (then and now) thought their kids could do no wrong, even when presented with airtight evidence. Not coincidentally, usually it was the parents who didn't want to hear it who had (and have) the real problem kids. But all the other parents in the neighborhood knew about these kids and kept a close eye on them.

I'm active in our Neighborhood Watch, which is an organization that is partly necessary because we have abandoned that social contract. Maybe it's time for us to recommit to the neighborhood parenting idea. We can start small, making a mutual agreement with the parents on our block – tell them we want to know if our kid is out of line, and that we'll thank the messenger, and that we'll do the same for them.

Sure, your kid might have a good explanation. But he also might be a 7-month-old puppy, long on energy and short on sense. And once that puppy gets off the porch, without help, we may never get him back, no matter how much we wish we could.

Retrospective Notes for *Puppy Patrol*
- Bailey is now nine years old. That means now I'm only 6 times older than she is (people years) instead of 79 times older.
- In those years, Bailey has slowed down and wised up, so she isn't the flight risk she once was.
- But I've slowed down even more, and she knows it, and she reminds me of that fact from time to time by grabbing a loose sock and out-maneuvering me until she's good and ready.
- Coincidentally, Daniel (now 21) and Madison (now 19) have wised up as well, even if they haven't slowed down.
- We were lucky enough that (knock wood) they chased any squirrels or anything else into serious danger.
- At this point I think any attempts to keep them on the porch would actually achieve the opposite, so we are trying not to try so much.
- I've seen the saying (and I wish I knew who wrote it) that "behind every great kid is a mom who is pretty sure she's screwing it up." Stacy and I both have our doubts about the job we've done, but we are hoping and praying our two great kids manage anyway.

TEEN TRAUMA
Originally published: August 2003

When I was a boy of fourteen, my father was so ignorant I could hardly stand to have the old man around. But when I got to be twenty-one, I was astonished at how much he'd learned in seven years.
                                            - Mark Twain

Parents of newly minted teenagers often seem astonished by the trouble, pain and unpleasantness involved in raising what they lovingly refer to as their "hormone-fueled... conflict-seeking... little... smart-mouthed... aaarrrgh... gack... gggaaahhhhhhhhhhhh!"

Why, the parents ask, does this have to be so?

The good news is that there is a logical reason for what you have to go through. The bad news is that the mountain-climber who hacked off his own boulder-pinned arm with a pocket knife to escape certain death also had sound logic behind him, but that doesn't mean it hurt any less.

To clearly understand this logic, it is helpful to consider, ironically, the process of pregnancy and childbirth. Since witnessing my wife carry our two babies to full terms, I have been convinced that the sole purpose of the tenth month of pregnancy (40 weeks of pregnancy ÷ 4 weeks per month = <u>10</u> months and <u>don't</u> <u>you</u> <u>forget</u> <u>it</u>) – from the unbearable discomfort to the impossibility of sleep to the humiliating number on the scale and even to the constant and unwelcome belly rubs from strangers – the purpose of all of this is to put the mom-to-be into a mental state of such profound discontent that she will do anything, *anything!*, to get that baby out. *NOW!*

Whether as a result of evolution or divine inspiration or both, the tenth month of pregnancy is *supposed* to be miserable, to make the inevitable and necessary pain of childbirth bearable. By my math, the same principle applies to parenting a teenager: it is *supposed* to be as difficult as it is. And once again, Darwin's theory or God or both have succeeded wildly.

Take communication – a key ingredient to healthy relationships. A parent has no more chance of understanding the meaning or motivation behind the next 20 words that come out of his teenager's mouth than he might of understanding the next 20 grunts that come out of the kid's CD player. The point is moot, however, since the parent is unlikely to get 20 words total out of his teenager between now and high school graduation.

Then there's music, which intersects with communication. How many times do you think *this* conversation has occurred?

Parent, snapping fingers gamely and vaguely in rhythm: "Hey, this band is good. Who is it?"

Teenager, disdainfully: "No Doubt."

Parent, gamely: "Yeah, no doubt! They're great? What's their name?"

Teenager, irritated: "No Doubt!"

Parent, confused: "Right, no doubt... but, um, what's their name?"

Teenager, exploding as she storms out: "YOU DON'T EVER LISTEN TO ME! GEEZ!"

I wouldn't be surprised if bands actually name themselves with an eye toward sparking these types of exchanges:

Parent, slightly gun-shy but still trying: "Uh, hi... Ah, this band sounds good too. What's their name?"

Teenager, still disdainful: "I Hate You I Hate You I Hate

You Don't Ever Talk To Me Again!"

Parent, confused again: "Yeah... uh... any chance I could see the album cover?"

Teenager: "*Album* cover??? God, that is so *20th Century*? You are SO LAME!"

Parent: "Is that, uh, really the name of the band?"

Teenager: "GEEEEZZZZ!!!!!"

And before you know it, these two formerly loving family members, who spent the last 13 years cuddling on the couch reading *Goodnight Moon* and playing checkers, now cannot *wait* for the kid to grow up and get the heck out of the nest.

Simply put, humans' survivability as a species improves when offspring of a certain age want to get as far away from their parents as they can. Sort of like those helicopter seeds riding the wind to a new sprouting ground far from the parent tree, except the seeds don't slam the door and curse the tree's name on the way out.

So there it is: a logical explanation, rooted in evolutionary principle, for why the teenage years – for parents *and* teenagers – are as difficult as they are. It is to make the inevitable and necessary separation of parent from child more bearable.

Feel better? No? Well that mountain man's stump probably still hurts too, but at least he's alive. And in five or ten years, he and you and your kids are gonna have some pretty good (but still slightly painful) stories.

Retrospective Notes for *Teen Trauma*
- So, you aren't going to like this: when I wrote this essay, my children were seven and five years old.
- In my first book (*Nose-Sucker Thingees, Weeds Whacking Back & Cats in the Bathtub: Does Life Get Any Better?*), I told a story about a young pediatrician with no kids who dismissively tried to tell me I shouldn't have felt bad when my kids cried when I wouldn't let them in our bed at night. I did not react well, and generally don't when

someone with no experience on an issue holds forth knowingly.
- I am not sure what hubris led me to think I should write about parenting teenagers when I had no experience.
- That said, I think I was right. ☺

PERFECT STORM
Originally published: September 2012

OK, I'll say it. We have lost our collective mind.

A perfect example is... well, any program on what used to be called *The Learning Channel*, but is now *TLC*, which I think stands for "Totally Lost Control."

We'll skip for now how disgusting it is that parents will put their kids on national television programs like *Toddlers 'n Tiaras* or *Dance Moms* and somehow try to say they are doing it for their kids.

OK, I can't skip that. If these parents were around in ancient Rome, they would have tried to get their kids a spot on the next episode of *Christians v. Lions* on the Colosseum network. The only things these parents (and *TLC*) are doing for their kids is permanently damaging their well-being and their ability to function as normal adults when they grow up.

But back to how these kidsploitation shows perfectly illustrate how we have lost our collective minds. On the shows, the parents and the teachers drill into their kids the expectation that they be "perfect." Meanwhile, the parents and teachers spend half the show cursing each other, waving their index finger from side to side, doing that head- / neck-bob thing, and telling the camera what's wrong with everyone except themselves.

It is this dichotomy of expecting perfection from others while ignoring our own imperfections (or, even worse, beating ourselves up for our own imperfections) that has become a hallmark of our society.

We push our kids to take all the right courses, and get great grades, and do all kinds of activities so they can get into the "right" college (as if there is only one right college) and so they can have the "right" career (as if there is only one right career, and as if they will have only one career). Then we wonder why our kids are so stressed.

Meanwhile, we ignore the fact that we (and when I say "we," of course, I mean "I") slugged our way through high school, quit half-a-dozen activities, graduated college with a two-point-oh-my-God-I-am-not-going-to-make-it grade point average, held half-a-dozen odd jobs before beginning a "career," and changed careers three times, sometimes by choice.

Yet we expect perfection from our kids. Why? To make up for our own imperfections? To compete with the perfect parents down the block?

We enrolled our daughter Madison in piano lessons. After many enjoyable years of that, Madison just wanted to play piano. It took me a while to figure out that you can play piano without taking piano lessons. Today Madison plays piano every day and she is happy.

We also expect perfection from others, starting with our political leaders. Believe me, I am no fan of our political leaders. But we want them to have led perfect, mistake-free lives, and *then* expect them to have the answers to the problems we face today. Guess what? You don't learn anything if you don't make mistakes. Someone who says he has led a mistake-free life is either deeply flawed or hiding something (or, more likely, both).

We (I) expect perfect customer service at all times. My son Daniel gets mad at me when I get grumpy at bad service.

"But I have to let them know when something isn't working right!" I counter.

"No you don't," he says. "And you could be nice about it if you are going to tell them."

You know, learning stuff from my kids takes the shine off that veneer of perfection I am trying to project to them.

Here is the truth: The opposite of "perfection" isn't "imperfection." The opposite of "perfection" is "normal."

Scottish writer Rev. John Watson (or possibly Plato or Philo – there isn't perfect agreement on the source) said, "Be kind. Everyone you meet is carrying a heavy burden."

I like that.

Now, some of you are probably saying, "Hey, Chuck, you weren't very kind to those parents on *Toddlers 'n Tiaras*!"

OK. You're right. But you have to draw the line somewhere.

Retrospective Notes for *Perfect Storm*

- I should have made a distinction in this essay between *Dance Moms* and dance moms. My sister Kathy is a dance mom. Both her daughters love dance, and participated for most of their lives. So Kathy has spent two decades supporting them, traveling with them, and hanging out with other "dance moms." That's a wonderful thing and an admirable sacrifice for a parent to make (same goes for parents of kids who truly enjoy pageants). There is a very big difference between making it possible for your child to do what she loves and forcing your kid into life-damaging situations on national TV just to satisfy your own twisted needs.
- In the years since I wrote this, Madison has developed and pursued a passion for photography and sculpture rather than piano, and is majoring in those arts in college. I would have been parental malpractice if I'd forced her to stay focused on piano and never given her the room to find her real life's passion. You can see Madison's photography at **http://photographybymadison.wix.com/welcome**

AND NOW A WORD FROM VALENTINE'S DAY

The next few essays are very Valentine's Day-specific. Every February I used to write a Valentine's Day column, and these are some of them. The points hold for any time of year, but if it makes you feel better to save these essays for post-Super Bowl reading, who am I to argue?

VALENTINE VALIDATION
Originally published: February 2004

Early February always brings an odd and confusing vibe to our house.

The flu usually has invaded our dwelling, while significant chunks of our savings have fled our accounts. Low gray skies and lower temperatures have driven our children in from the outdoors and to each other's throats. Chores put off during the rush of November and December suddenly loom like the wind-driven waves of a winter nor'easter in the eyes of my wife, Stacy. It causes her no end of worry and fret.

And amidst all the emotional turmoil, Valentine's Day blinks in the near-distance like a lighthouse on a jagged, rocky shore. Like a tipsy Exxon tanker captain, I get a nagging feeling that I have a problem but I have no idea what it is, exactly, or what to do about it.

So I turn to the expert: Dr. John Gray (he came after Dr. Ruth, but before Dr. Phil), of Mars and Venus fame. His diagnosis: Generally, women feel simultaneous and equal pressure from all unaddressed issues, even if some of the issues are not actually important. Generally men, conversely, prioritize and weigh tasks, determine the most important one, and feel the pressure of just that issue.

Blame it on the Neanderthals: Prehistoric woman learned she couldn't afford to focus on just one child, allowing the other half-dozen to be picked off by saber-toothed tigers, woolly mammoths or hedgehogs the size of bison. Meanwhile the male mind followed a different evolutionary route (which, by the way, had nothing to do with refusing to ask directions – we chose this path as far as you know). The successful knuckle-dragging man needed only to kill a single mammoth or hedgehog. Focus on one thing at a time, get it done, and then we're done.

Squeeze both world views into one modern house and conflict ensues. Defusing this psycho-emotional fusion bomb has consumed more resources, person-hours and wood pulp than the Manhattan Project.

The solution, apparently, has come down to this: Change the men.

But most of us men are OK with that. Guys (generally) want to reduce the stress on their wives. All we need is some training. Classical conditioning. Stimulus response. Like Skinner's rats or Pavlov's dogs, we're pretty simple animals really, and we're willing to learn.

But the best technique that pop psychology has had to offer women is the empty adage uttered ad nauseam by everyone from Oprah to Abby to Phil Donohue: "There's nothing sexier than a man doing the dishes."

Hah! Has any guy ever gotten the sugar cube after vacuuming, or changing the baby, or cleaning the litter box? Ever? As Pavlov's slobbering dogs could tell you, all bell and no cookie does not the trick teach. Instead you end up with a belligerent old hound laying on the couch, emitting foul odors and growling at requests to get off his butt.

And, yeah, occasionally we screw up the tasks. I remember once joking, while visiting my brother Ken's house, that Stacy clearly didn't think I'd remember to bring back a rake that Ken had borrowed. She even called to remind me while Ken and I were talking about it.

It was humiliating. It was insulting. It was ridiculous. It was about a 50-minute round trip when I had to go back to Ken's house later that day.

But here's the point: We have no idea what we're doing. We want Valentine's Day to go well – really. But evolution left us a few pages short of the whole story, and we won't figure it out before next week.

So just give us the list. Tell us: Get these things done by Feb. 10 and we'll do our best. Simple.

Of course, also keep in mind another old saying: You are allowed to tell a man what to do, or how to do it, but not both.

Do those rocks sound closer to you?

Retrospective Notes for *Valentine Validation*
- I had to do some significant clean-up on this essay. It was even more convoluted and confusing than it is now.

FOR THOSE KEEPING SCORE AT HOME…
Originally published: February 2008

Heads up men: the high holy day of St. Valentine's Day is approaching.

Women don't understand the anxiety that this holiday creates for men. It's worse even than tax day, because at least we know what the government wants from us. But women? We understand nothing: not how women think, their choices, motivations, likes or dislikes – NOTHING.

Men are like the blindfolded guy who touches a section of the elephant but can't fathom its entirety. Except the elephant is actually a rodeo steer and when the guy carefully reaches out to touch the steer, the steer gores him or stomps him or throws him into the third row.

The fact that I chose a metaphor using elephants or steers to represent women only confirms the problem.

From men's perspective, if making a woman happy were a multiple-choice test question, none of the options would make sense:

Question: What do women want?
A. Indigo
B. 3
C. Who's on first? I don't know! THIRD BASE!!

This wouldn't be a problem, except most men really like women and want women to like us back. But we don't know what will make women like us.

So we guess. Our first guess: a woman wants a man who treats her well. WRONG. It turns out that girls often want the bad boys. Makes no sense, right? Actually, from an evolutionary standpoint, it does. Back in the caves, the males fought over the female, then the female went with the biggest and baddest to ensure the strongest possible offspring.

Sure, he's a ticking time bomb, but he's irresistible. That's no consolation to us non-NFL players (or those who cite Darwin to explain our lack of appeal to women), but at least it's logical.

Then there's the scientific literature (i.e. trashy novels). These books feature a heroine driven crazy by the hard-muscled, hard-to-figure, hard-to-love, impossible-not-to-love rebel/stud detective or whatever, who gives her the cold shoulder one moment and rips off her bodice (whatever that is) the next.

The problem: hard-to-love is about the best that most guys can do. And without the rest of the package, hard-to-love is pretty hard to love.

Then there's the challenge of a long-term relationship. Hillary Clinton said it well – not about marriage (insert joke here), but about politics and governing. Knocking charismatic Barack Obama, she said, "One campaigns in poetry but governs in prose." It's the same with romantic relationships: courtship's poems are nice, but they don't change the diapers, take out the trash or scoop the litter box.

It's not easy to be Barack one moment and Hillary the next as you struggle to keep a marriage romantic and rolling. (For Republicans uncomfortable with the Barack/Hillary marriage metaphor, feel free to swap in Santorum and Romney, but I'll bet you're still uncomfortable.)

Problem is, in a relationship you must constantly run for re-election. Otherwise, you'll find your spouse flirting with some attractive Independent candidate, sort of a Gary Johnson without the geography issues.

Sound complex? Well, try figuring it from a man's perspective. We are, justifiably, not known as the more discerning, nuanced, perceptive half of the species.

Despite the complexity, I DO know what I DON'T want: a relationship based on torment, tests and traded insults. In that vein, my wife, Stacy, and I have come to at least one positive conclusion: don't keep score.

Men, if your wife says she wants a girls' weekend, don't say, "Well, then you owe me a boys' weekend!" Instead, say, "ABSOLUTELY! In fact, make it a three-day weekend – me and the kids will be fine." Pull your goalie and make it easy for her.

And women, don't wait for your husband to call in the debt – instead, you suggest he deserves a guys' night out.

As I write this, my wife and her friends are cavorting at the beach on a girls' weekend. And I am sure Stacy soon will offer to cover at home while I go do some guy thing.

Regardless of your approach, you'll get yours, and she'll get hers. The question is whether you take it from each other or give it to each other. Even a guy can figure out which is healthier.

So this Valentine's Day, give her some jewelry, sure – but throw away the scorebook.

Retrospective Notes for *For Those Keeping Score at Home*...
- I did some research when editing this essay for the book (something I usually studiously avoid unless an editor is a stickler for accuracy). While Clinton did say about Obama, "You campaign in poetry. You govern in prose," it was Mario Cuomo who said it first. But acknowledging Cuomo would have made the joke too long (imagine: Mario Cuomo making a passage too long!), so I left him out. ☺

- The "attractive Independent candidate originally was Ross Perot, but his name recognition today is slightly better than John Tyler (or Mario Cuomo).

LOVE DOESN'T HAVE TO BE A DISASTER
Originally published: February 2009

It's time again for the annual Valentine's Day column. Like most stories about love, this year's Valentine's Day column begins with a tale of natural catastrophe and massive destruction.

I've lived long enough to have survived the San Francisco earthquake at the age of 27. No, not the 1906 San Francisco earthquake, you smart aleck. I'm talking about the 1989 World Series earthquake. I went to graduate school in San Francisco and happened to be there when "The Pretty Big One" hit on Oct. 17, 1989.

It was a sunny, fall afternoon, the San Francisco Giants and the Oakland A's were just taking the field at Candlestick Park for Game Three of the "Bay Bridge World Series," and like most guys in their 20s, I was settling in to type a college paper for my girlfriend (who somehow had never learned how to type) (or drive, somehow) (but at least she had the initiative to pursue a college degree in her mid-20s) (although now that I think of it, all this talk about a former girlfriend is probably not contributing to a positive Valentine's Day this year) (OK, back to the earthquake story).

So there I was, not watching the World Series at 5:03 p.m. I had just finished a long stretch of typing when, remembering what my high school computer science teacher always told me ("Mr. Hansen, please stop drawing pictures of Evel Knievel jumping cars and pay attention..."), I hit "save" on the big, square Commodore 64 computer – this was before most people had picked that first Apple from the tree in the Silicon Valley of Eden. Deep in the innards of the machine a couple of prehistoric hamsters started running on a granite wheel, stirring the napping mini-pterodactyl and prompting him to use his beak to chip the contents of the screen onto a stone computer disk.

A couple seconds later, the 7.1-magnitude earthquake hit. It felt like God had picked up the building and was shaking it like a Yahtzee cup. As my chair was tossed sideways and I spilled to the floor, I saw the computer monitor crash down off the table and bounce across the room like dice. "Thank God I saved!" I immediately yelled, according to the story I tell my kids (which isn't entirely true) to convince them to save their homework (which they ignore).

However, this isn't a story about frequently saving your work on your computer (although you ought to, because YOU NEVER KNOW WHEN AN EARTHQUAKE WILL HIT). You and my editor are probably wondering what this story is about. I'll tell you in a minute.

Anyway, the biggest California earthquake since 1952 hit, but thankfully I had been in the Golden State for a year or two, so I was well versed on the correct actions to take during a temblor (a fun word): Do not run from the building since debris may be falling in the street; get under a solid structure like a thick table or desk; stay away from breakable stuff like windows, china cabinets, etc.

And here's what I did: I jumped to my feet and staggered across the heaving floor past a solid wooden table to the window, which I threw open and looked out (knowing full well I was three stories above the street – not sure what the plan was there), then ran around in circles for a few seconds (it was a long earthquake), then dashed from the apartment, down the undulating staircase (another fun word... undulating, not staircase) and out into the street, where cars were swerving out of control, and power lines were falling.

In short, in spite of all I'd learned, I did everything I was NOT supposed to do, and nothing that I was supposed TO do. My rational brain had ducked under some solid structure in my head, and my instinctive, irrational brain had taken over. About the only idiotic thing I did *not* do was put a big glass vase on my head and juggle knives on my way down the stairs. I was very lucky I wasn't hurt – lots of people weren't so lucky.

There are two Valentine's lessons here for me. The first is obvious: When an earthquake hits (geological or emotional), I've learned not to react instinctively and make the situation worse (for example, by jumping out a third floor window or to irrational conclusions). Usually the best reaction to a significant upheaval is to slow down, think through my next steps and try not to lose my head. It can be counter-intuitive in the moment, but when the yelling starts, that's a good time to stop yelling. My wife, Stacy, is very good at that – the more upset I get, the calmer she gets, and in response, the calmer I get.

The second lesson is more about cause than effect. The earthquake was the result of slippage along thrust faults formed by compressive stresses where two continental plates collide. In relationship terminology: Issues that had gone unaddressed for too long, finally caused a destructive argument. Sometimes when stresses are building between Stacy and me, we *try* to release the pressure a little at a time – maybe in somewhat less emotional discussions – so that when the breaking point is reached, it causes less damage. The challenge is that this requires us to regularly raise difficult issues (in rational tones) as they come up, and that is uncomfortable. However, the alternative is to stay silent, defer the discomfort and add the issue to a growing list of frustrations that inevitably will spark a "Pretty Big One."

Neither approach is easy, but you have to take one or the other. On that fall evening in 1989, some friends and I drove around the city, and the damage was almost inconceivable. Buildings were burning, bridges were collapsed and sirens wailed. Late that night, I looked down across San Francisco from the high point of Twin Peaks and saw the entire city dark, except for the raging fires.

I know which approach we'd take geologically, if we could. Why not do that emotionally, since we can?

Retrospective Notes for *Love doesn't have to be a Disaster*
- Nothing to add.

THE ONE-SIDED POWER OF LOVE
Originally published: February 2011

Men dread the middle of February, and not just because the Super Bowl is over, and baseball season is a month and a half away.

The reason: Valentine's Day. Look, we went Christmas shopping for our wives just 59 days ago (do the math), and now we have to do it again?

To these men I say: What's wrong with you? Valentine's Day is the ultimate celebration of how good men have it in life!

In the game of love, men are always the Harlem Globetrotters, and women are always the Washington Generals.

Blame it on the power of love. Blame it on evolution. Blame it on God (but do it tactfully, you know, just in case). But the result never changes: Women are stuck with men. It isn't fair, but that's life.

And it really isn't fair. I mean, look at us men! We're uncommunicative. We're typically smelly and often disgusting. We're hairy and getting hairier, except ironically on our heads. Not every older man is hairy, but that's just because they work at it. In truth, there comes a point in every man's life when he starts getting razor cuts on his ears, and not because the razor slipped up there from his cheek.

Poor women. How did this happen?

There is the theological perspective: In the Old Testament, Adam and Eve eat of the forbidden fruit in the Garden of Eden (it's not productive right now to get into a he said-she said-He said on whose idea it was). God punished both, but Eve got the worst of it – not only would she now have to endure painful childbirth, but God said that in sorrow (and I quoteth) "thy desire shall be to thy husband."

That's right: God's punishment for women was that they would desire their husband! And they call Him a merciful God?

I'm sure there are examples from other religions, but my deadline for this column was last night, so I'm going to push on.

There's also evolutionary grounding: Recently the Washington Post reported that "when kissing, a woman is attracted to a man who smells like he has different immunity DNA." For example, men are not immune to making rude noises, but are immune (generally) to shopping, as in: We HATE to shop. I'd rather watch *The View* than shop. And I'd rather chop off my toes with a cold butter knife than watch *The View*.

So blame it on DNA, which stands for "Don't (got) No Alternative."

Finally, there is the power of love, a theory introduced by Dr. Huey Lewis in 1985 and reinforced seven years earlier by Scott Peck in, his book *The Road Less Traveled*, in which he describes the irresistible, tsunami-like – but temporary – feeling of falling in love. Thank God for temporary insanity!

So it's a lock theologically, genetically and pop culturally. This is why an otherwise sane man would incur the Pajama-Gram (mail-order sleepwear) TRIPLE risk: 1. Giving unmentionables (presumptuous); 2. Guessing on the size (I don't know my own sizes); and 3. Mail-ordering said unmentionables (making the inevitable mistake unfixable).

Yes, love is a wonderful thing.

Especially for men.

Retrospective Notes for *The One-Sided Power of Love*

- My editor thought "disgusting" was too strong a word to use when describing men. That editor is a woman. Classic Stockholm Syndrome.
- Now, in 2015, the "Washington Generals" reference has as much relevance to most readers as a Martin Van Buren reference (who, for the benefit of those same readers, was neither a Washington General nor a piece of furniture).
- I wrote this in 2011 and, in 2017, *The View* inexplicably is still on the air.
- Regarding my reference to Genesis 3:16 and the sorrow of God making women desire their husbands as punishment, my editor wrote me and said, "I'm not sure that's what that means…." See, this is the problem with some editors: They are always so insistent on accuracy, or at least reasonable interpretation. Honestly, it gets in the way of making a point sometimes.
- In retrospect, I should have added additional information on how insane it is for a man to order pajamas for his wife by mail order.

THE FRUITS OF LOVE
Originally published: February 2005

St. Valentine's Day is nearly here, and that calls for a love story. Like all love stories, this one begins with a good bachelor party – mine. And it doesn't end there.

It was 11 years ago and the best bachelor party I'd ever attended. For this, I thank my brother Ken, his meticulous planning and his utter disregard for the security deposit he'd put down to secure a large conference room at a nearby hotel. The observance included several kegs, along with equipment for a wide variety of indoor and outdoor sports, including whiffle ball, Nerf football, Frisbee and lawn darts (the last two actually ended up as part of the same game).

During the festivities, my friend Donnie approached, hefting a large melon of some sort in one hand. "You know what this is?" Donnie asked, grinning.

"No," I mumbled.

"This here's something you're gonna get real familiar with," Donnie drawled. "This here's a honeydew melon."

I stared at him blankly, not just because I didn't understand, but because I was staring blankly at everyone at this point.

So he threw it at me.

I didn't catch it then, and I haven't done a great job getting a handle on it since: the Honey-Do List.

I really don't give the Honey-Do List the attention it deserves. I've never finished the attic (but in my defense, I didn't start the attic). I haven't sealed the deck in a while or painted the porch. It might sound like I'm lazy, but in fact, I'm just religious.

See, I believe God invented money for a reason. And that reason is the Honey-Do List. It's not just me, either. My friend Darryl, who is of a different faith than I, shares my core tenet, believing God invented money to hire guys to take care of his lawn. Ironically, Darryl lives in the West End of Richmond, where giant houses are packed so tightly that Darryl needs a lawn service like Charlie Brown needs a hair stylist. Regardless, Darryl does not store up the fleeting treasures of this world. Instead, he gives them to a lawn service so he can go play golf.

Who am I to question God's wisdom in this matter? Unfortunately, it is often the holiest who are least understood – in my case, by my wife, Stacy. She disagrees with my interpretation and has on the rarest of occasions even implied ever so obliquely that my religious fervor might be closer to sloth than saintliness.

Yet Stacy loves me. Even after 11 years, two houses, and dozens or perhaps hundreds of Honey-Do Lists that have yellowed and wilted and crumbled away on the bulletin board, with not a single task crossed out, she still loves me.

And to her credit, I have never once come home from work to find a van parked out front bearing the slogan, "Handyman Inc.: We do the Honey-Do jobs that your honey won't do." (They might as well add "if you know what I mean" to the end of that marketing gem.)

Yes, it's true love, despite all my faults (including my deep spirituality). We've thrown off the curse of the melon that was hurled at me 11 years ago, and we remain happily married. It's a real-life love story and a fitting tribute to the potency of St. Valentine (and the power of money).

Retrospective Notes for *The Fruits of Love*
- Today, as I edit this essay, Stacy and I have been married for 23 years and one day.
- I have backslid a little bit from my deep spirituality, getting a little better at the Honey-Do List, but not enough for a reasonable wife to be pleased.
- Yet Stacy has stuck with me, against all odds (specifically, the betting odds set by my friends, pre-marriage), and I am the luckiest guy in the world.

BEN AND JERRY AND VALENTINE'S MONTH
Originally published: February 2012

The other evening I was chatting with my lovely wife, Stacy, when I shut my mouth suddenly – not because I was out of words (of course) but because a large, un-chewed chunk of food that had been hiding in my mouth since lunch was about to fall out my face, mid-sentence. This happens to me, seriously, all the time.

About seven years ago I noticed an odd little numbness on the left side of my nose. Within a few months, the numbness had spread to most of the left side of my face, from my eye to my jaw, and including the left halves of my lips and tongue. My muscles all work fine – I just constantly feel like I'm coming off of Novocain.

I've had the thing checked out and the neurologists can't really nail down a cause. They just know that whatever is going on, it isn't killing me. So I try to ignore it.

This mostly works, except after I eat, because if some food sneaks up into the space between my gum and my cheek and I can't feel it, I won't realize it's there until it makes a surprise appearance. Perhaps during one of my (hopefully humorous) speeches.

Nothing undermines – or enhances, now that I think about it – the humor of a speech like a fully intact peanut falling out of your mouth while you are talking.

The other problem with this numbness thing is my taste buds don't work as well on the left side, so the joy I used to get from a pint of Ben & Jerry's ice cream has been reduced. (Why I'm not skinnier by now I have no idea. Well, I have a few ideas.)

And that brings me to Valentine's Month.

(Well, it's Valentine's *Day*, technically. But not for long, because right now medium-powered lobbyists for certain greeting card companies are up on Capitol Hill, doling out campaign donations and buttonholing congresspersons and senators. The goal: Convince Congress to use the state's power of *eminent domain* to condemn the presidents' birthdays and force them to relocate elsewhere on the calendar, leaving February clear for commercial development as Valentine's *Month*.)

You can't swing a dead Pepé Le Pew on TV right now without hitting some clever man at a restaurant presenting his honey with a bauble (purchased from the correct store), which always leads to his honey abruptly calling for the check and throwing the man onto the table for some instant positive feedback.

Here's the thing about Valentine's Day: It is built on the idea that *someone else* is going to come in and make you feel loved. But that won't work if your capacity to feel loved is diminished, in the same way that a pint of Ben & Jerry's can't make you happy if your taste buds don't work right.

Unlike with our taste buds, however, there are things we can do to raise our self-perception of our worthiness of being loved. Start by being aware of that critic in the back of your head who is always telling you how worthless you are. Author Rick Carlson put a name to this little monster in his classic book, *Taming your Gremlin* (which I highly recommend). Other taming techniques from Carlson include:

- Breathe! Your breathing both reflects and regulates your level of contentment.
- Feeling good is primarily an inside job. Events occur *around* you. Your experience of those events occurs *within* you.
- Your past is not attached to you. You may be holding onto it. But it is not holding on to you.
- Your Gremlin always wins a wrestling match, but hates just being noticed. Simply notice your thoughts, feelings, fantasies, memories and assumptions – positive or negative – and notice that the real you is not any of these.

So, while gifts from your significant other on Valentine's Day are nice, it's also nice to give yourself a gift: the permission and the ability to feel worthy of being loved.

(There are limits. Our dog Bailey will lick the floor where food might have fallen out of my mouth two days ago. If your emotional taste buds are that developed, you might be a little *too* willing to accept love, if you know what I mean.)

It's also a good idea to avoid letting food fall out of your mouth during that romantic dinner. It really takes the shine off the bauble.

Retrospective Notes for *Ben and Jerry and Valentine's Month*
- The left side of my face is still numb.
- And, earlier this year, the right side of my face went numb too. I got it checked out again, and we still don't know why it has happened on either side.
- Still not dead from it though.
- I still eat Ben & Jerry's. In fact, I ate half a carton last night. I'm an idiot.

THE BIG OCEAN OF MARRIAGE
Originally published: February 2013

February has a men's holiday (the Super Bowl) and a women's holiday (Valentine's Day).

I say this for two reasons. One: I want to generate some letters to the editor, and if that means I have to drive women to protest that they like football or men to insist that they like Valentine's Day, so be it. (But, seriously men... I mean, seriously?)

My second reason is to introduce my annual Valentine's Day column, which this year is about how we often romanticize marriage and how blissful it is supposed to be. That is not to say marriage isn't blissful. It is! (Or can be.) But there's more to it.

In his song *Mañana*, Jimmy Buffett sings, "Don't try to describe the ocean if you've never seen it." Years ago I spent five weeks crossing the Atlantic on a 51-foot sailboat. Prior to the trip, I had preconceptions about the ocean (mostly from movies and television). But after a couple of weeks on the North Atlantic on our boat *Jaska*, I began to understand Buffett's point: you may *not* know what you think you know... about the ocean, and other things.

My most surprising discovery about the ocean was that it could be utterly still and flat, without a ripple or a whisper of wind. On these days, we could look over *Jaska*'s rail and see a perfect reflection of ourselves in the ocean.

Other times (usually when a storm was a few hundred miles away), the ocean undulated beneath us, with hundreds of yards separating the rounded tops of each eight-foot swell. This teased the inner ear – I could sense *Jaska* rising and falling, but my eyes reported flat seas.

More frequent were short, choppy waves. Day and night for the first week out of St. John, we plowed through four-foot waves that seemed to come from ahead, astern and either side, all at once. I didn't eat much that first week.

Most exhilarating were days and nights with moderate seas of six or seven feet, a good breeze and clear skies. But there also were times when the ocean was exactly as you've seen it in the movies – steep swells of frothy gray sea water, irregularly spaced and rolling powerfully by.

How *Jaska* rode these 15-foot waves depended on luck and timing.

If we happened to slide down the backside of a wave at the right time, we might smoothly roll up and over the next one. But if the previous wave set us down at a funny angle, the next wave might catch us with our rail down, and explode like a colossal water balloon along the length of the boat. The result: several thousand gallons of cold, dark ocean water crashing across the deck, sweeping into the ocean anything – or anyone – that wasn't tied down.

Handling the wheel in these conditions was nerve-wracking, and sleeping could be difficult. One night I awoke to the feeling that *Jaska* was suddenly tilting upward. And she was, as we climbed a steep wave. As we crested the wave, *Jaska*'s pointed bow pitched sharply downward. Our cabin was toward the front of the boat, so as my bunk cushion fell away from beneath my body, I briefly floated in midair. Then the angled underside of the bunk above smashed down, crushing me like a hanging curve ball and sending me rocketing across the cabin.

The ocean – and for that matter, marriage – can be many things: choppy, rolling, exhilarating, terrifying, even as flat as glass. Sometimes several of these simultaneously.

However, often a young couple expects continual wedded bliss (like in the movies), and then they are surprised by difficulties. Thinking their marriage is failing, they abandon ship rather than riding out the storm.

Marriage is a big ocean, with many different faces – including occasional stormy weather. And surviving the journey becomes even more meaningful when you overcome challenging situations together.

So don't generalize about marriage because, as Buffett warns, "you just may wind up being wrong." But feel free to generalize about men and women and how they feel about football and Valentine's Day. Particularly if you're looking to generate letters to the editor.

Retrospective Notes for *The Big Ocean of Marriage*
- This column did not generate a single letter to the editor. Not one. Draw your own conclusions, but none of them are good.

BOOM. IT'S VALENTINE'S DAY
Originally published: February 2016

Here's the problem with Valentine's Day: it takes advantage of men.

Men don't get a lot of sympathy from culture these days, understandably. There's no doubt that we still have it pretty good. Just open a Fortune 500 annual report to the board of directors page or compare the lines for the men's and women's bathrooms at any large event and that becomes obvious.

So I'm not crying nobody a river about this, but still… Valentine's Day is a massive commercial holiday built on the weakness of its target consumer: men.

It's the equivalent of a pontoon boat bobbing around in the ocean where minutes before the Titanic had been floating… selling life rings for $2,000 a pop.

It's like showing up on Mars and offering Matt Damon a ticket back to Earth for the low low price of just everything he has in his pockets plus his entire checking account plus half of his credit card limit.

Actually, now that I think about it, that would be a good deal for a stranded astronaut but it's a hell of a lot to ask from some palooka who's busting his ass every day just to put food on the table and keep a roof over his family's head.

Nonetheless, for men, doing Valentine's Day right is vital, but we have no idea how. When it comes to Valentine's Day and (what we think) our honey expects, men are at sea. We are in a totally alien environment. (See how I did that?)

So what do the jewelry stores do? They offer to help.

- They offer coded guidance; for example, "He went to Jared!" means "She wants you to go to Jared, you moron, so her friends [supposedly] will be impressed."
- Or they give you a romantic idea, like walking ten miles up and down two mountains in three feet of snow to stomp the shape of a heart into the frosted hillside. She'll love it!! But, the jewelry store warns, despite the fact that you risked death by elements or grizzly on this dreamy gesture, she still expects jewelry.
- Or they create a special line of jewelry, like a bracelet with matching charms that go on it, which means it's *the gift you keep giving*, because there are a billion different charms and clips and clasps and whatnots that match it. So it's like buying a piece of jewelry on an installment plan that never ends.

When I go into the jewelry store, I double park because I'll be back in my car in less than five minutes. I'm sure I'm going to make a mistake so I might as well make it quickly and get on with my honey-do list.

Amazingly, however, Stacy has always loved what I picked out. In fact, the odds of her loving every gift I've given her over two decades are so astronomical that…

Well, let's just say that maybe the best Valentine's Day gift has been the one she's given *me*, 25 years in a row, when she's managed to say, "Oh, this is beautiful! I love it!"

Retrospective Notes for *BOOM. It's Valentine's Day*

- I wrote this less than two years ago. I have no retrospective thoughts yet.

AND NOW BACK TO GRIPING ABOUT AGE, KIDS, DOGS, ETC.

OLD MAN, LOOK AT YOUR LIFE
Originally published: November 2012

Paula Broadwell and Mother Nature recently faced off, and Broadwell won.

If you don't know Paula Broadwell, she is the biographer, writer and philanderress who, in full partnership with philanderer and retired Army Gen. David Petraeus, managed to compromise the integrity of the CIA and wreck, or significantly damage, at least two families.

I say at least two families because the resulting brouhaha has also ensnared Gen. Petraeus' successor in Afghanistan, Marine Gen. John Allen, who is being investigated for potentially improper communications with the socialite who went to the FBI after Broadwell sent her threats from Petraeus' email account...

Good grief, it's impossible to keep the generals and the generals' not-wives straight without a program.

You know the Pentagon brass is having a tough month when the good news is that a *third* general has been caught up in an ethics scandal, but at least *this* general was behaving inappropriately with his *own* wife. (Gen. William "Kip" Ward got in trouble for extravagant expenses he incurred from flying his wife with him all over the world on the government dime.)

When it comes to Petraeus and Broadwell and the general infidelity epidemic, frankly it is amazing to me it has occurred at all. Mother Nature, for many reasons (all related to the survival and propagation of the species), has stacked the deck against these sorts of dangerous liaisons. All things being equal, Mother Nature is rooting for the young bucks, not the bucket lists.

Want proof? Look in the mirror. More specifically, look in MY mirror. What do you see? I'll tell you what *I* see: a mobile hair farm. I regularly cut my *ears* shaving, and it's not because my razor blade accidentally strays way up there. It's because I'm 50 and Mother Nature is making sure that when young women look at me, they think: "hedge clippers."

That's fine. I love being 50 years old and married.

In fact, I really wouldn't mind if Mother Nature were intentionally making me a *little* less attractive. But Mother Nature is going all out. My beer gut is bordering on keg gut. Hair is sprouting out of my ears and eyebrows and back like a time-lapse video of grass growing. Meanwhile I had to shave what was left of the hair on my head so that no one would think I am under any illusions.

My gums are receding with abandon, to the point where I'm expecting my teeth to just drop right out any time. Until then, those teeth are getting smaller and crookeder and yellower. My head is expanding like a Macy's Thanksgiving Day Parade balloon, and my eyes, nose and mouth seem to be huddling in the center of my face, terrified by the horror show going on around them. And then... *then*... there is Old Man Smell.

I really have to admire the genius of Mother Nature. I also would like to tell Mother Nature something, and that is this: Enough!! THAT'S ENOUGH! MISSION ACCOMPLISHED! DO YOU HEAR ME MOTHER NATURE? OBJECTIVE ACHIEVED! YOU CAN STOP! LAY OFF!

Then I look at Petraeus, and I think: Despite all that, Broadwell and he still got together. Henry Kissinger once said that power is the ultimate aphrodisiac, and it must be true. It would *have to* be to enable Broadwell to ignore the Old Man Smell.

Retrospective Notes for *Old Man, Look at Your Life*
- Apparently I really liked that "cutting my ears while shaving" joke. That's the second time I've found it in an essay and I'm only half done editing this book.
- I mentioned a couple of other generals who were the subjects of investigations when the column ran. Here's how those turned out:
    1. On January 22, 2013, General Allen was cleared in a misconduct inquiry. He retired from the military in April 2013, but continued to work as an advisor to Secretary of State John Kerry and then-Defense Secretary Chuck Hagel.
    2. In 2012, General Ward was stripped of a star and allowed to retire as a three-star lieutenant general. Ward also was ordered to repay the government $82,000.
- As I write this, *right now*, I have a little piece of tissue stuck to my ear, hoping it will clot a self-inflicted hemorrhage.

DOGS, PRIDE AND KIBBLE
Originally published: June 2010

"Pride goeth before destruction, and a haughty spirit before a fall."
— *Proverbs 16:18*

I admit it. I used to be a dog snob.

I used to judge people not by the content of their character, but by the behavior of their dog. If your dog barked uncontrollably, jumped on people, pulled food off tables and out of mouths... well, you were just a poor excuse for a dog owner.

Not only that, I'd extrapolate my judgment to the dog owner's parenting skills, and sometimes even verbalized these self-righteous condemnations.

So, if the miracle of Google has brought a certain past girlfriend to this particular column, please tell your parents I'm sorry about what I said about Max (and, by extension, about your parents).

Pride does indeed go before the fall.

Our wonderful dog Bailey, a slim, graceful, playful 50-pound Labradoodle, is DRIVING ME OUT OF MY MIND. She eats shoes (only the ones I like). She'll eat anything she can reach on the counter, whether food or paper or plastic or checks or cash. She eats school books and television remote controls (nine so far at $18 a pop). We finally started putting the clicker in a box, so she began eating cordless telephones and cell phones.

Ironically, we keep food in her bowl at all times, and she doesn't eat much of that... probably because she's so full.

She barks at anything that moves and lots of stuff that doesn't.

We've tried a dog trainer. The trainer was good – so good, in fact, that I will not reveal her name here out of fear of ruining her reputation. Thanks to this trainer, we know exactly what we aren't doing right. Call it user error.

Yep, pride goeth before the fall, and I have fallen a long way since my prideful judgments on others based on their dogs' behaviors.

But whether it's the dog's fault or our fault (and if I were a betting man...), I am learning a valuable lesson from Bailey: You can't always control the ones you love.

I've also learned something else from Bailey: Love cometh before the pride.

As I mentioned earlier, we keep Bailey's food dish full all the time. But if I grab a handful of Bailey's kibble and call her, Bailey will sit next to me or at my feet, waiting patiently as I slowly hand-feed her.

Even when her full food bowl is just a few inches away, and Bailey could quit begging and feast at any time, this not-always-obedient dog prefers to sit quietly, waiting for gifts from me.

Love cometh before the pride.

In our media-saturated world, a person can find reinforcement from virtually anywhere. But nothing means more than loving gestures from someone we love.

Think about that next time you have an opportunity to pass along a verbal hug to a loved one who might not *seem* to need affirmation from you. It may mean more than you know.

Retrospective Notes for *Dogs, Pride and Kibble*

- Bailey, now nine years old, has settled into mid-life. She no longer eats shoes or remotes or phones. But she still loves to be fed by hand, and she has grown more cuddly and affectionate as she's aged. Now Bailey is like a warm, furry, soft, breathing pillow, and I love to sleep with her curled up next to me.
- In one of those painful life paradoxes that seem inescapable, though, I miss the young Bailey, and I feel guilty for wishing she'd grow out of her puppyhood.
- But I don't miss the destruction.

YARD YARNS AND FISH STORIES
Originally published: August 2010

So I was out mowing the grass in the dark tonight and a neighbor walked by, pointed at my push mower and asked, "You got a light on that thing?"

"No," I replied. "I just don't care if I cut straight."

Fact is, if you lower your standards a little, you can pretty much cut the grass any time day or night.

This can be a very helpful realization.

Sure, my lawn might look like the turf-equivalent of a Picasso painting, but let's be honest – I'm not exactly a candidate for the Scott's Lawn Care Hall of Fame. My dog has dug so many holes in our yard that we wear ankle braces when we go outside. I edge so infrequently that by the time I get around to it, gravity and erosion have combined to extend my hillside yard halfway down across the street.

Often I'll miss a week of cutting the grass due to some emergency, like the fact that there are fish in the lake. But the grass continues to stubbornly insist on growing, *even though* I was generously giving of my time to show largemouth bass that there is a big, beautiful world above the lake surface.

So the next week I'll plow through the overgrown savanna, flushing rabbits and pheasants and antelope and generating tons of grass clippings.

Lawn experts say leaving clippings on the yard helps retain moisture and produces a healthier stand of grass. Whatever. All I know is it takes a LOT less time to leave the clippings then bag them.

Of course, cutting a lawn neglected for a week (in the cause of expanding the horizons of the noble black bass) produces rows of clippings, browning in the sun and prompting the legitimate question (to me, anyway) of whether the yard looked better with overgrown grass.

It's not just the yard either. I wash my car so infrequently that when I finally do clean all the dirt off I get a nice bump in gas mileage. By shaving once every two days, I not only save three minutes every other day, but I also cut razor costs 50% and lose half as much blood.

You may laugh (I mean, you have permission. Go ahead.), but three minutes multiplied by 182 days (rounding down) is nine hours a year.

That's nine hours during which I can be playing with my kids (in three minute bursts, I guess). Or talking to Stacy. Or walking the dog. Or exercising. OK, forget that last one.

It's about priorities. That's no slam on folks whose priority is cutting grass so it can grow back. After all, one of my priorities is to pull fish out of a lake and then put them right back in again.

But time is the only currency that really counts in life. You get only so much in a day, a year, a life. It may mean that my yard sometimes looks like I cut it wearing a blindfold, but I'll take that over missing time with Stacy, Madison, Daniel, Bailey, family, friends and fish – not always in that order.

Retrospective Notes for *Yard Yarns and Fish Stories*
- I'm an IDIOT. All that time I could have been wearing a headlamp when I cut the grass in the dark.
- Now my lawn is neatly cut (not that I care), and there's more time for ~~fishing~~ family!

GRAVITY, CHANGE AND THE ROLLING STONES
Originally published: May 2008

NOTHING is more predictable than change. And NOTHING seems to take us so consistently by surprise.

How many times in December, January and February do I find myself saying this in a conversation: "Can you believe how cold it is today? Man, it is so cold! Can you believe it?"

...And *I really mean it*! WOW, it's so cold, it's like it's.... WINTER.

I'll sit on my porch in the thick heat of our Virginia summer, and I cannot fathom the distant, hazy tree line as anything but green and full and sweaty. And yet... six months later the trees are naked and I'm saying idiotic things like, "Jeez, can you believe how bleak the woods look?"

Here's the thing about change: Saying we need to learn to "cope" with change is like saying we need to learn to "cope" with gravity. Change isn't something that Al Gore invented during the 1990s when he had nothing else to do. Change is like the Rolling Stones... it has always been part of existence, and it always will be.

In fact, I wouldn't be surprised if change is one of those elemental aspects of the universe, like time or light, and that one day some little Einstein will crack the code on change, translating it to mathematic equations and creating yet one more school subject in which the world's kids kick our kids' butts.

No, it's not change we need to learn to cope with. It is ourselves that we need to learn to cope with.

"But Chuck," I hear you whine, "change is really, really hard! I don't like it!"

Yeah, well, I don't like how much effort it takes to pull myself up from the couch, walk into the kitchen, yank open the freezer door, wrestle the lid off a pint of Ben & Jerry's, and then walk all the way back to the couch again. But that New York Super Fudge Chunk ain't gonna float over to me. Gravity (not an optional part of life) is keeping that ice cream where it is and it's going to fight me every step of the way over to the fridge. But there are some things you just gotta do. Neither gravity nor change (nor, apparently in my case, Ben & Jerry's) is optional.

Parenting is a great example. "Well, I just don't know what's gotten into him," the parents of a pre-teen or teenager will say when the kid gets all sullen over some (seemingly) minor issue. And we mean it! We're stumped! "What happened to our little boy?" As if: A. we have never heard of the concept of cranky, independence-craving teenagers; and, 2. we never were teenagers ourselves.

So we fall, mindlessly, right into the pattern: resenting the resentment, yelling about the yelling, banging on slammed doors, and on and on. The teenager's bad behavior shouldn't be excused, of course, but for God's sake, we shouldn't be so surprised. Gravity. Change. The IRS. Cute toddlers turning into grumpy teenagers. Get used to them. They're not going anywhere.

My brother Ken and his wife KT have always worked to push themselves emotionally forward, redefining their roles as parents in anticipation of the maturing of their kids, so that they never find themselves parenting a teenager like he or she was a toddler. Ken will be the first to tell you they haven't always been successful (although I will tell you they've been pretty damn successful), but at least they're aware of the issue and are trying.

I remember a colleague who brought her four-year-old son into work one day. They were buying a candy bar from the coffee cart, and the kid wanted to grab the candy from the cart himself. His mom stopped him mid-grab, scolding, "No! Mommy do! Mommy do!"

I swear, she said, "Mommy do." Most four-year-old boys who heard that would think Mommy was using some hilarious bathroom language. Four-year-olds are pretty far beyond Spaghetti Western Injun' talk, but this mom was still the parent of a two-year-old in her mind and in her actions.

We invest a lot of emotion in the way things are, and even more in the way things used to be. But (supposing for a moment that ol' Al Gore is right), chaining ourselves to the way it is or used to be is like buying coastal property that's already 10 feet under the rising waters' surface. Unless you're going to build SeaLab 2020, you need to do some more thinking.

Retrospective Notes for *Gravity, Change and the Rolling Stones*
- I was a little too enthusiastic about all caps back in 2008.
- As we go to print, the Rolling Stones are still not dead.
- I'm sure some of you are grumpy about my Al Gore jokes, but: 1. I've heard scientists say that, whether climate change is real or not, Al Gore was the first person to win the Nobel Prize for a PowerPoint deck; and, 2. I've heard scientists say that politicizing climate change was the most counter-productive move imaginable if you truly wanted to solve climate change. So, you know, there you go.
- Kenny and KT's kids turned out GREAT.

SLIPPERY SLOPE
Originally published: February 2006

It has been one of my metaphoric maxims in life: Don't shovel the walk while the snow is still falling. In other words, why put work into a task if you're just going to have to do it all over again shortly thereafter? You might as well wait, and shovel the walk once and well.

This philosophy is part laziness, part practicality and part *carpe diem*. There are so many things you can do with the limited time you've been given. Why waste it doing the same job more than once when you don't have to?

Our house is on a little plateau on the top of a little hill.

Side note here: Actually, when we were negotiating with the builder for the house, I tried to say that the price should be lower because the house was on a hill. The builder looked at me like I was an alien from the planet Idiot.

Anyway, we like our little hill. Sure, the driveway is pretty steep, given that the garage entry is not very far from the street. But we drive up the driveway, not walk up it. Who cares how steep it is, right?

Well ... as it turns out, during the winter, the sun spends most of its time in the southern half of the sky, granting our north-facing driveway only a brief, glancing dose of light, and then only in the cold, early-morning hours.

Therefore, when we get snow or ice, our steep driveway turns into the kind of icy Black Diamond ski slope that has broken the leg of many a Virginia skier.

Oh, sure, it can be funny. There was the snow storm the night of Super Bowl X?X!, some years ago. A friend tried to come over to watch the game, but wound up repeatedly, awkwardly sliding slow-motion to the bottom of the driveway, first on her knees, then her butt, then her stomach and finally her back, flopping around like a fish on a steep frozen driveway. She only got off the slick angled pavement by crab-walking sideways to the snow-covered lawn, finally staggering into our home with her sense of humor intact, if not her reputation for grace.

Then there are the many times we've ignored winter storm warnings from a frenetic John Bernier and parked our cars at the top of the driveway. And in 10 percent of those cases, we've ended up with a driveway so icy-hard, slick and steep that getting the cars down again was more like tobogganing than driving. More than once while descending that icy hill I've prayed that our SUV would capsize on the way down rather than slide uncontrolled out into traffic.

See, it turns out that the longer the snow sits on our driveway, the harder ultimately it is to get off. That's because the bottom layers of snow turn to ice, hardening and melding to the driveway like cooling lava. If I don't get the snow off the driveway as soon as it begins to accumulate, it's there until March.

Back in early December, as I shoveled snow off the driveway only to watch a couple billion other beautiful, unique and infinitely aggravating snowflakes take its place, I thought about how I've had to abandon my maxim of "Don't shovel the walk while the snow is still falling," at least when it came to my driveway. I enjoy a good metaphor as much as the next guy might enjoy a triple banana split. But sometimes in life, that particular maxim misses the mark.

In some areas of life, the longer one takes to clear off the collecting icy problems, the slipperier and more intractable those problems become. Yeah, the snow and ice may still be falling, and you may end up out there shoveling 10 times a day, and even then it may feel like you're always losing ground.

But if you don't get out there in the snow and ice and sleet and crap and keep shoveling, then you will never have a chance, and you'll end up in the SUV of life, sliding down the hill with no steering, no traction and no options, hoping that the thing will capsize rather than take out your mailbox. Metaphorically speaking, of course.

Retrospective Notes for *Slippery Slope*
- Who is John Bernier, you ask? John has been a ~~weatherman~~ meteorologist here in beautiful RVA (Richmond, Virginia) for as long as I can remember. John appears on WRIC Channel 8 nightly, but is never more enthusiastically resplendent than when there is threatening weather on the horizon.
- John once showed up on the air for a major snow storm dressed in a tuxedo. I am pretty sure it was not New Year's Eve. I think he dressed up in the tuxedo because he was excited. I may be wrong, but that's how I remember it.
- In any case, that's who John is, and as far as I can tell, he's no more accurate than the ~~weatherpeople~~ meteorologists on Channel 6 or Channel 12, but he dresses better.
- This is not an essay about shoveling the driveway.

WHAT UP, CUZ?
Originally published: July 2013

Stacy and I are getting an early preview of empty-nest living. Daniel and Madison have been out in Idaho the last few days visiting my sister Linda's family, and they won't be back for a week or so.

To avoid screwing it up, I will just say: so far, so good.

I wasn't worried, of course. But, you know...

OK, that's probably enough.

I am *definitely* not worried about whether the kids are having fun in Idaho, because they are with two of their cousins. There are nine cousins total in our family, ranging from 9 to 21 years old, and they are *tight*.

Cousins are like siblings without the instinctive rivalry. They are a solid sub-unit within any family, and it is wise not to pit their loyalty to each other against their loyalty to the larger family.

Several years ago, on our annual family beach vacation in Sandbridge, Virginia, the ten adults were sitting around the kitchen talking while the nine cousins were off in another room playing. Actually, eight of the cousins were in another room. Charlie, the oldest cousin, then 16 years old, was in the kitchen with us.

We adults were commiserating about the idea of going to the go-cart park up in Virginia Beach the next day with the kids. This place has five or ten go-cart tracks, some inner-tube bumper boats, a couple little roller coasters.... that kind of thing. The place is fun when you go with a bunch of friends, or when you are a kid. But when you are a parent taking your kids there, the go-cart park becomes the world's biggest and most expensive paved frying pan (Disney parks excepted).

Given what you pay for two kids to race on a handful of go-cart tracks, you ought to be allowed to take the go-cart home with you. The food prices would make an airport vendor blush. Somehow they seem to have angled the pavement in the park in such a way that it focuses all of the sun's energy on you, no matter where you stand. And every six minutes an F/A-18 Hornet roars over the park low enough to count the pilot's nose hairs (yes, I love jet noise, and God bless America, but jeez they're loud).

Again – no problem with friends. But… Hell with kids.

So we began plotting ways to get out of going – we'd tell the kids that the track is closed this week, or that there was a go-cart recall... anything to avoid another torturous year.

All the while Charlie just sat at the kitchen table, hand in his pocket, taking in the conversation. I think I said something to him along the lines of, "Now that you are older and one of us adults, see what we have to deal with?" Charlie just smiled.

Seconds later, all eight of the remaining cousins came rushing in from the other room, yelling about how much they wanted to go to the go-cart park tomorrow. Their entrance could not have been timed better—it blew our scheming out of the water. But their timing was not coincidental, as we figured out when Ben, the youngest cousin, blurted out, "Charlie told us to come in here and talk about the go-cart park!"

Charlie had no-look pocket-texted the cousins with the warning of what was going down, even as he looked me right in the eye.

I was stunned. "I thought you were one of us!"

Charlie stood up, still smiling, and said, "I am, and always will be, a Cousin first." Then all nine cousins went down to the beach to play.

Retrospective Notes for *What Up, Cuz?*
- It's hard today to describe how impressive Charlie's texting trick was.
- This occurred back in the days of the flip phone. Today, with touch-screen phones, I'm not sure it would be possible to pocket text.
- That said, it was no easy feat back then. If you recall, the keyboard on a flip phone was the telephone key pad, so in order to text, you had to punch a key a certain number of times to get to the right letter. For example, to type the letter "C," you had to punch the "2" key three times. It's confusing to explain and I can see what I'm typing.
- So I am still in awe of Charlie's pocket-texting performance.
- More than that, I am proud of Charlie's priorities and loyalty.
- But I'll be damned if I'm going back to that go-cart park again.

AMUSEMENT PARK MUSINGS
Originally published: September 2008

Recently I took my two kids, Daniel and Madison, to Busch Gardens, along with my nephew Christian and a friend of Madison's. All the way down to Williamsburg I regaled them with tales from the late 1970s when I spent three glorious summers working at King's Dominion – surely a teenager's dream job if there ever were one.

For me, that first real job at King's Dominion was as much about independence as it was about money. At $2.35 an hour it had to be.

I remember riding in a 1960s-era jalopy up Interstate 95 (a road barely 20 years old at the time), the big red sun rising in the east to the sounds of Jackson Browne's *Stay* or Styx's *Blue Collar Man*, donning ridiculous pastel shirts and berets and trooping into Deutsche Treats on Kings Dominion's International Street, where we'd put in 40 hours of minimum-wage work every week, and we LIKED it.

It's never a good sign when you realize you sound like Dana Carvey's parody of a grumpy old man. But I can't help it – I'm old. I'm so old, when I worked at King's Dominion the Lion Country Safari had actual saber-toothed tigers. My manager was a Neanderthal. Our cars had stone cylinder wheels and holes in the floor instead of gas and brake pedals.

There we were, a bunch of 16- and 17-year-old kids working in an amusement park full of thrill rides, junk food and other 16- and 17-year-old kids. Through hormone-induced fogs, we scooped ice cream, made donuts and generally provided atrocious customer service as we focused mainly on making each other laugh. Then we'd get off work and go into the park and play until closing.

As I stepped through the Busch Gardens gates many years later with my own kids, almost immediately my son conjured that instinct for independence. "Can Christian and I go off by ourselves?" he asked.

I considered the request. Daniel is 12, and his cousin is 13. On one hand, I understood their desire to strike out on their own. On the other hand, the network evening news magazines and Nancy Grace have succeeded in scaring me to the point that I'm afraid to let the kids out into the *backyard* without an armed guard. Taking a deep breath, I nodded assent and handed Daniel $60.

I kept 10-year-olds Madison and her friend with me though, and both tolerated my presence admirably. We checked in with the boys a couple of times during the day, but I really didn't interact with Daniel again until 5:30 p.m., when he called to say he was out of money.

To Daniel's credit, though, he and Christian had thoroughly enjoyed the spending. He described a "feast" at the Octoberfest Hall that included pizza and French fries and chocolate cake and Diet Coke (gotta watch those calories…).

Given the food prices at Busch Gardens, which are just shy of what it would cost to actually fly to Europe for lunch, he probably spent a good amount of money in the beer hall (just like his old man…).

But they'd also found an arcade game they could beat consistently and, pouring in quarters, milked it for all it was worth. Christian and Daniel then cashed in the tickets they won for novelty items like whoopee cushions and trick gum. You might be thinking that Busch Gardens got the better end of the deal, but if you recall when you were 12, whoopee cushions and trick gum were worth their weight in gold, and they kept us laughing all the way home.

As we drove back to Midlothian, I thought about how great getting a taste of independence felt when I was a kid, and I was glad that Daniel and Christian were able to enjoy a day of it. And I thought about the independence that awaited all of these kids just a few years down the road.

Some things don't change. The older they get, the more independence kids want from their parents, and an amusement park is still a great place to get it.

Retrospective Notes for *Amusement Park Musings*
- Busch Gardens should have paid me for this one.

AXLE-DEEP IN PARENTING
Originally published: January 2009

I was witnessing a classic teenager/father-of-a-teenager moment. A friend of mine out in Powhatan County had called me for help, and now I beheld the situation in its full, awful and eventually hilarious glory. I was standing at the top of a hill under a power-line alley, looking down through the fading light of a cold winter afternoon into a muddy, brush-covered valley.

Wedged into the bottom of the sloppy hollow was a big mud truck, looking like a half-dead dinosaur stuck in a tar pit. Midway up the hill between me and the doomed monster was a much smaller pickup, wheels spinning in futility on slick Piedmont clay. A frustrated middle-aged man (my friend) sat, half in the driver's side of the cab, looking back at a teenager (his son) as the young man pushed with all his strength on the bed door of the small truck.

The situation was immediately clear. The teenager had been out trail-busting the night before with his buddies when he got his truck stuck. Apparently the vehicle was in deep (and so was the kid), because you know that boy must have tried every possible way of getting the truck out before resorting to asking his dad for help. Eventually he'd bitten the bullet, and now the worst possible thing had happened: his dad had gotten *his* truck stuck trying to get down to the *son's* stuck truck.

I had been in the situation before, albeit not in my current, much more comfortable role. During my tumultuous teenage years and young adulthood, a significant percentage of my biggest mistakes ended up with Dad having to drive somewhere he didn't want to go. I won't list the places I made him come to, since it would immediately convey what my big mistakes were, and I'm still trying to fool my kids into thinking I was perfect growing up (the fact that they read my columns notwithstanding).

Suffice to say that each mistake was big enough that the guaranteed downsides of involving my father were outweighed by my need to have his help in extricating myself from the situation.

What I didn't realize at the time of my transgressions was that the situation was harder on my dad than it was on me. Sure, I was in trouble. I was going to lose car privileges or be grounded or have to pay possibly hundreds of dollars to make things right. And I had disappointed my parents, which at various times caused me varying degrees of emotional discomfort (I am ashamed to admit I wasn't always devastated). But my problem was one-dimensional.

From my perspective now, as a father, though, I can see that Dad's situation was multi-dimensional and much harder. He was TICKED, absolutely, and he was going to make sure I was punished for my buffoonery. But he also likely was relieved – relieved that my idiocy hadn't gotten me injured or worse (this time). And I'm sure he also was not surprised. The unfortunate fact is that people do stupid things on a pretty regular basis, and teenage boys' crimes of stupidity are especially predictable.

It isn't easy to be angry, relieved and unpleasantly unsurprised all at the same time, and then to be able to act in a way that addresses the situation appropriately. It completely explains the seemingly nonsensical statement: "Thank God you're OK. Now, when we get home, I'm gonna kill you!"

You are angry as hell and still love them. You are going to get them out of trouble and then they are going to be in a world of trouble. I get it now.

So I felt for my friend's son, who in his obvious, red-faced humiliation had to help push his dad's truck out of the mud that he'd gotten his dad into. But I really felt for my friend, who was going to have to drive through some more complicated and conflicting issues.

Fortunately for him, the current predicament was presenting opportunities for doing that. For example, it was made clear to the son that he'd be washing his dad's truck that night no matter how cold it got. And more than once I think my friend hit the gas, not to move the truck, but to throw some more mud back onto his son.

I wish we could make some New Year's resolutions for our kids that would keep them (and us) out of these situations, but I'm afraid we have to rely on our kids instead. We've done our best to get them on the right path, and now all we can do is pray for the best and be ready to pull them back onto that path (and make sure they pay a price) when they stray.

At the same time, it doesn't hurt to remember that while we parents don't get our cars stuck in the mud anymore (or not very often, anyway), we still screw things up, sometimes spectacularly. So perhaps our resolutions should be for patience with our kids, humility for ourselves, and a prayer for guardian angels all around.

Retrospective Notes for *Axle-Deep in Parenting*
- I like this one.

YOU HAVE TO CRAWL BEFORE YOU CAN CRAWL
Originally published: September 2010

I witnessed a charming scene in a fast-food place the other day. A young mother was leaning in close to her one-year-old child, cooing and giggling and gently encouraging her to speak. "Mama?" the mother whispered to the little girl. "Mama?"

"Ba-buh," replied the child, drooling and laughing.

"Mama?" repeated the mother patiently, even joyfully.

"Ba-buh!" said the baby.

Well, actually, I am only guessing that was what they were saying. I couldn't really hear them over the crystal-shattering racket of a two-year-old kid on the other side of the restaurant shrieking, "MAMA! MAMA! MAMA! MAMA! MAMA! MAMA! MAMA! MAMA! MAMA! MAMA! MAMA!!!!!!!!"

Of course, the two-year-old was only half the conversation. His mother was also shrieking (the nut doesn't fall far from the tree), "WHAT?! WHAT?! WHAT?! WHAT?! WHAT?! WHAT?! WHAT?! WHAT????!!!"

Some challenges of parenting are one-step-forward, two-steps-back. Other challenges, however, are one-step-forward, 10-steps-forward.

Teaching a kid to talk is one of those. We spend a year trying to get a child to speak, and then the next 10 years trying to get them to stop.

When I was a kid, my favorite game was asking, "Mom, guess what?"

"What?" she'd answer.

"That's what!" came the punchline.

Pause three seconds.

"Hey mom, guess what?"

It's a wonder she didn't lock me in the closet. More often. It's not until the stormy teen years strike that parents get a reprieve, and of course then they complain because kids refuse to talk.

Walking is the same thing. The work that parents put into teaching a kid to walk is dwarfed by the effort that is required once the kid is mobile. If I had it to do over again, I'd tell Daniel and Madison that, as Irish-Norwegian-Anglos, it is our cultural tradition to crawl on our tummies without using our legs.

Yes, it would have looked goofy in public, but at least at home we could relax for 30 seconds before a kid got into trouble.

Last week, my brother and his wife experienced the most poignant of these parenting paradoxes. After 18 years of guiding, teaching, consoling, cajoling, punishing, encouraging and nurturing, their older child – no longer a child, of course – has stepped out of their home, off to college.

Charlie is exactly who the phrase "fine young man" was coined for, and he is an exemplary role model for my two kids. Ken and KT have done a great job as parents, and their bittersweet reward is seeing Charlie head out into the real world, or at least to college.

One-step-forward, 10-steps-forward.

Of course, if Charlie is really smart, he'll teach his kids that, as proud Irish-Norwegian-Anglos, the world is best seen from tummy level.

Retrospective Notes for *You Have to Crawl Before You Can Crawl*
- Charlie is now a fine young college graduate and professional, still setting a great example for my kids.

MY LOUD, IRISH, NEW YORKER THANKSGIVING
Originally published: November 2003

It's that time of year again, when defenseless, quiet souls – doomed creatures that would never hurt a living thing – are sacrificed at the Thanksgiving dinner table. Tragic.

It's tough being an in-law in the Hansen family. My family – parents and four siblings – is a chaotic blend of Irish-Catholic immigrants and type-*HEY!* personality New Yorkers. My Mom had 11 brothers and sisters, and was raised in a home where happiness increased with the number of family members in a given room at a given time. My Dad and his four brothers and sisters grew up in Brooklyn, where even the most routine dinnertime discussions registered 100 decibels-plus: "*HEY! PASS DA BUTTA!*"

Then, in 1964, AMF transferred Dad and his young family to Richmond. Our degree of Southern acclimation may best be illustrated by this fact: Each sibling – assertive, gregariously argumentative and comfortable in a crowd – chose a spouse who is shy and polite, averse to crowds and loud situations and, most of all, very Southern.

We did not surrender all northern characteristics, though, and Exhibit A is our Thanksgiving dinners. In contrast to Southern celebratory suppers, where the grandfather clock's venerable tick-tocks are audible two rooms away, and the silverware rises silently from cloth napkins to squeak and slide across family china, my family's holiday dinners are mind-numbingly loud cacophonies of arguing and laughing and shouting and chewing. That's right – we chew loud.

Here's a Thanksgiving dinner recipe for you: Mix well-mannered Southern in-laws with expressive northern extroverts. The result is a culture conflict that leaves "My Big, Fat, Greek Wedding" looking like Miss Manners' family reunion.

It's hardest on the in-laws, of course, as the following true story illustrates. Out of sensitivity to the in-law in question, she will go nameless, except to say that I have one brother and it wasn't my wife.

This sweet, quiet girl was at her first Hansen Thanksgiving dinner. She was nervous. Real nervous. Bunny-dropped-in-a-kennel nervous. So, to help her feel more comfortable, we offered to include her in the pre-meal blessing. Counter-productively, we chose the alphabet blessing, in which each person around the table sequentially takes a letter and thanks God for something that begins with it. "A: thank you God for these apples." That's right – twenty-six different, sequential "Thank-you Gods."

The good Protestant girlfriend was not comforted, however. Instead, she was panicked senseless, and she sat paralyzed, too scared even to count one letter ahead and think of a ready answer. Meanwhile, the blessing marched onward: "B: thank you for our brothers and sisters. C: cranberry sauce from a can (*hey, that's a double!*)."

The girl's time to speak drew inexorably nearer. "D: this delicious meal."

There was just one Hansen between her and her moment of truth. Her mind was racing, with her heart just steps behind.

"E: excellent conversation."

All eyes then turned expectantly toward the trapped young maiden. It was her turn. F. F was her letter. F. F!

She felt dizzy, her ears buzzed and her eyes darted around the table. What started with F? Potatoes... no! Butter beans... No! Turkey? No! *Nothing!*

An idea sprang forth through her desperation: Use an adjective! Use an adjective that starts with F to describe something, to describe the turkey! The "what" turkey? The F, f, f, f, f, f turkey. No F-word would come to mind!

Worse... one F-word *did* come to mind! And that was the one F-word she couldn't use!

Until her boyfriend, her future husband, the father of her future children, the man who had gotten her into this mess to begin with, began snickering...

We never got to G. Probably just as well.

Retrospective Notes for *My Loud, Irish, New Yorker Thanksgiving*
- It can now be told. That sweet, demure Southern gentlewoman was, and still is, the beautiful, wonderful Kathleen Turner (KT) Hansen, Kenny's wife.
- And she gracefully puts up with the retelling of this story every Thanksgiving.

MOTHER'S DAY?
Originally published: May 2012

For an old man, I have a lot of friends and coworkers who are expecting or who have just had a baby. And I always have the same reaction (in my mind) when friends tell me they are expecting: "How can you have a kid when I'm so tired?"

I say this in my head because our evolutionary imperative to reproduce makes it *verboten* to divulge exactly how hard it is to have and raise kids – especially at the beginning.

The problem with this unwritten taboo against spilling the Cheerios is that young parents *believe* us, and when parenting turns out to be hard (SO HARD) they feel like failures.

So evolutionary imperatives be damned, I'm gonna shoot straight here.

By the way, my degrees are in mass communications and public affairs, so I have absolutely NO qualifications to make the following assertions. On the other hand, Dr. Phil has a degree in philosophy, Dr. Laura has a degree physiology and Dr. Johnny Fever had a degree in spinning records, so I am going to plunge ahead.

To start with, when you get that little alien... I mean your bundle of joy... home from the hospital the first night, it is going to scream from 7 p.m. until 6:45 a.m., then pause for 15 minutes just to raise your hopes, and then scream from 7 a.m. until 6:45 p.m., and then repeat the process. For two months.

We actually called the maternity ward the first night we had Daniel home at about 2:30 a.m. because the creature... I mean our beloved son... was inconsolable, which made three of us. Actually, Stacy called the hospital. I was in the attic looking for a nice picnic basket so we could leave him on someone else's doorstep. (OK, that's not true.) (But the thought may have occurred to me.) (Briefly.)

We eventually figured out that the screaming meant either he was hungry, had gas or had dirty diaper. But as soon as you learn how to handle one issue, another one will pop up.

For example, there are the baby-raising purists, always out there circling, judging, throwing guilt trips. Baby-sleep purists will tell you that not letting the baby cry himself to sleep is a form of abuse. Breast-feeding purists will say that if you don't breast-feed until the age of... well, you saw the *Time* magazine cover... then you are dooming the kid to a shortened life of extreme allergies. Formula purists will demand you feed your kid the hyper-expensive formula from the politically correct, Third World-friendly company or you are an elitist monster. The solution for these people: ignore them. They'll move on to the next crop of new parents soon enough.

The cost isn't entirely emotional, of course. For example, trips to our parents' houses turned into massive logistical nightmares, as we jammed our suddenly tiny four-door car with the critical baby toys, stroller, carrier, food, diapers, clean-up materials, medical supplies, spare clothing, etc. At that point, the only difference between you and a frontier family humping all their worldly possessions across the country in a wagon is you're not dragging a mangy mule and you don't have arrows in the side of your vehicle.

Then there are the financial costs. You might have heard it takes about $175,000 to raise a child today. What they don't tell you is that you spend $100,000 of that the first two years on diapers and formula. I could casually change a poopy diaper in the blink of an eye, but *buying* diapers made me cry. Formula is so expensive it should have flecks of gold floating in it.

All this is not to say there aren't rewards to having kids. When you have a baby, a chamber will open in your heart that you never knew existed. Your life will take on a new purpose and meaning that transcends nearly every goofy dream you ever had. And as your children grow and begin to lead increasingly independent lives, the mix of pride and bittersweet regret at the passage of time will take your breath away.

So, young folks, by all means, have kids. We *need* you to. But forewarned is forearmed, and God knows you need to be forearmed going into this gig.

One final bit of advice: if *Time* magazine asks if you are "Mom enough" or Tom Cruise ever tries to tell you there is no such thing as post-partum depression, you have my permission to knock them upside the head with your diaper bag. And be sure you have some cans of that expensive formula in there – you might as well get your money's worth.

Retrospective Notes for *Mother's Day?*
- I have heard from people I respect that Tom Cruise is the nicest guy you'd ever want to meet. But it's hard to get past that post-partum depression thing.
- I italicized *verboten* because it's a different language, not because I wanted to appear highfalutin. But that was the result, I am aware.
- I had no idea highfalutin was spelled that way until I just looked it up.
- I think *highfalutin* ought to be italicized.

YES WE TAN!
Originally published: May 2010

In case you are wondering, I finished spreading our mulch last weekend, which means it took me only four weeks to distribute 12 yards of mulch. That means my MulchFit age is 78 years old, which is two years younger than my WiiFit age.

I do have an excuse though (for my MulchFit age... there is no excuse for my WiiFit age). April 9 was our sixteenth anniversary, so Stacy and I took a long weekend to Sanibel Island, Florida.

Legend has it that on Sanibel Island Jimmy Buffett wrote his classic song *Margaritaville*, in which he famously could not find his lost shaker of salt (note to JB: check at the FDA headquarters in D.C.).

Brother Jimmy also sang that he was "Nibblin' on sponge cake, watchin' the sun bake... all of those tourists covered with oil..."

I'm glad Buffett wrote the song in 1977. If he wrote it today he would be "watchin' the sun bake... all of those tourists covered with SPF 75 sun block..."

I'm no 63-year-old singer-songwriter, but that doesn't sound as lyrical to me.

Song lyrics aside, we all now are well aware of the dangers of the sun (and red meat and eggs and coffee and alcohol and sugar and anything that doesn't either taste like dirt or taste like dirt was just washed off it). My dermatologist has cut me and froze me so many times that my skin hurts just driving past her building. In my convertible.

All that said, the beaches of Sanibel Island are still crowded with tourists looking for that perfect tan, but doing it safely, which is like looking for an invigorating cup of coffee with no caffeine.

Laying and playing on the beach over this recent long weekend, however, it dawned on me that, whether you are a beach baby from the '70s or a lotion-drizzled sand pastry from the '10s, if your goal at the beach is getting a tan, you may be missing something.

Moths, rust and thieves may not be able to take your tan, but time can and does. Days after you return from the beach, the tan fades and the treasure is lost.

Laying like a beached Stay Puft Marshmallow Man on the sands of Sanibel Island, it occurred to me that the pleasure wasn't in the tan that I'd leave with on Sunday and lose by Thursday, but in the time I was spending at that moment listening to the breaking surf and wondering with Stacy what the retiree with the metal detector might find.

For the record, I did not support Stacy's idea of throwing a handful of pennies out onto the beach to give the guy something to get momentarily excited about.

Digging my toes into the cool sand, though, a thought struck me that might be worth pondering almost any day: am I focused on acquiring things that will fade away, or am I focused on the joys and blessings of this very moment?

Retrospective Notes for *Yes We Tan!*
- Nothing to add. ☺

LOST IN CENTRAL PARK
Originally published: November 2014

Last month I took my daughter Madison and a friend of hers to New York City for a family visit and a photo adventure. That's right: The Big Apple, the City that Never Sleeps, the Town that Traffic Laws Forgot.

The ticket notwithstanding, we had a great time. The main event of the weekend was a surprise 80th birthday party for my uncle Jack McNally, a legendary private eye (trail attorney F. Lee Bailey's go-to guy) and former New York cop, which meant that the party was anything but a surprise. We had a wonderful night celebrating with my dad's side of the family, as we always do. New Yorkers can be hard-bitten and brusque, but when you're family, you're loved. Kind of like Olive Garden, but less cheesy and better food.

The photo adventure involved miles of walking through lower Manhattan, from Ground Zero to City Hall to Chinatown to Little Italy and back. It also involved a lot of car travel, which is where Madison and her friend – both approaching driving age – were treated to a clinic of how not to drive. The lane markings are merely suggestions there, and taxis swarm like honking hornets. We actually saw one taxi with bumpers around the entire car.

Central Park was the centerpiece of the adventure, and especially the Central Park Zoo where, for $12, you can look at a photograph of a deceased polar bear in front of the giant enclosure he used to occupy. Poor Gus the Polar Bear died a month before we arrived, killed either by natural causes or George W. Bush, depending on whom you ask.

But there was ten times more to the zoo than just no polar bear. At the snow leopard's cage, we saw the distant furry back of what a zoo worker insisted was the big cat sleeping in tall grass. I asked the worker how sure we were the snow leopard was even still alive, given what happened to poor Gus. The zoo worker didn't have an answer, or possibly was speechless.

We saw tiny tortoises trying in vain to crawl into the desert landscape painted onto the back wall of their small tanks, and in the aviary we had the opportunity to be pooped on by some of the world's rarest and most exotic birds. My favorite bird, though, wasn't in the aviary – it was in a giant aquarium. It was the penguin.

In the water, the penguin swims faster and more gracefully than most birds fly. Yet this bird spends most of its time and effort on land awkwardly practicing its odd gate, waddling around with its wings extended and its chest thrust out. The penguin seems to be following the advice you sometimes hear regarding self-development: work on your weaknesses. To me it makes more sense to build on your strengths and become the best person you were born to be.

That's why the most enjoyable part of the weekend for me was to watch Madison practicing and improving upon her gift of photography. We are all born penguins, with talents and with weaknesses. In a month when we give thanks, it seems almost ungrateful not to make the most of the best of what we were given.

Retrospective Notes for *Lost in Central Park*
- Poor Gus.

SUN AND COLD AND BALANCE
Originally published: March 2010

First of all, for the record, I have stopped hoping for snow. So any snow from here on out is someone else's doing.

Secondly, and this is related, it is ironic that the most important time to hear a positive perspective is when it's hardest to accept it, or even to listen to it.

Take the weather... (insert Henny Youngman joke here).

As Richmond-native and music superstar Jason Mraz sings in "Life is Wonderful": It takes some cold to know the sun; it takes the one to have the other.

But as we slide into March like a car (mine) sliding down a frozen driveway (again, mine) and into a mailbox (Uncle Sam's, but I have to fix it), the last thing I want to hear is that it takes some cold to know the sun.

Or, put another way: WHERE IS THE SUN ALREADY??

And that is the reason the song is so good. (As a side note, my friend Donna knows Jason's mother so that makes him and me nearly lifelong buddies, but I'd tell him straight if I didn't think the song was good. That's just the kind of friendship we have.)

When I'm looking at a mailbox half under an SUV, I may be grumpy but I still need to have that hope that things will get better. And I also need to hear that it's not abnormal to lose hope sometimes.

A few months ago, I was laid off from my job. I can't really complain though – the business rationale was clear, I wasn't the only person affected, and the company treated me well. Lots of people laid off from other companies haven't been so lucky.

Plus, I've always believed that challenging times are an opportunity for growth. Besides, how would we recognize the good times if we didn't have the bad times as a comparison?

Despite all this, sitting down to the hard math of expenses and savings accounts and how long until I have to have a job – it sometimes knocked the hope right out of me.

Stacy and the kids will tell you it sometimes also knocked the nice out of me.

After one particularly grumpy afternoon, I called my brother Ken (the smartest guy I know – even smarter than Jason). I was upset that I wasn't living up to my own ideals of treating challenges as opportunities, and was getting short-tempered in the process. Ken's advice was two-fold, and it turned me around.

He didn't tell me I needed to look on the bright side – at least he didn't at first. The first thing he said was that, given my situation, it was normal to be grumpy sometimes, and that I should cut myself a little slack. There will be good days and bad days and that's just the way it is. As he said this, I felt a weight lift from my shoulders.

Then he said that if I kept doing the right things, the situation would turn around.

And it's true. Everything can work out for the best (you have to work at it though) and there always will be ups and downs, cold and sun – it is all balanced.

In January I was lucky enough to land a new role with my old company, and so for now things are good again for us.

But for the many folks still dealing with challenges: I hope you will hang in there, accept that there will be some tough days, and remember that in everything there is balance. Things will get better.

Except for my mailbox. That sucker's history.

Retrospective Notes for *Cold and Sun and Balance*
- Seven months after this column ran I lost my job again.
- This time, instead of a month, it took 30 months to find another full-time gig.
- During that time I took a run at becoming a public speaker, a sort-of motivational humorist. While I had some success, I just couldn't reach escape velocity to make speaking a full-time job that met our financial requirements. But at least I took a shot.
- Meanwhile, though, it was 30 months of scrambling, taking temporary jobs and consulting jobs to make ends meet.
- Following Kenny's advice, I cut myself a little slack (but not too much) for being grumpy occasionally, and kept trying to do the right things.
- Thankfully, in 2013, I landed a new job that was even better than the ones I'd lost in 2009 and 2010.
- I'm not a fan of the saying "Everything works out for the best." I don't think that's true. Everything *can* work out for the best, but you have to make that happen through effort. It's not going to just come to you.
- And even when you do everything right, it still may not work out for the best. But if you gave it your all, then that's all you can do.

MID-LIFE CATHARSIS
Originally published: July 2010

If you've seen my wife Stacy lately and noticed a look of alarm, it is for a reason. I am showing classic signs of a mid-life crisis.

For example, I recently cut my hair, and not just a little. Imagine using a bulldozer to mow your lawn. My hair is shorter than that.

It doesn't help that my haircuts are self-inflicted. After my initial trim to scalp level, I bought an electric clipper, and now I'm saving $25 per haircut, and offsetting the savings with the cost to my career when I show up at work every two weeks looking like I passed out in a fraternity house the night before.

I look like my grandpa, except balder.

Stacy is *thrilled*, of course.

Not really.

I, on the other hand, have been surprised, particularly by the shape of my head. I knew I had a cleft chin; I didn't realize I had a cleft head. There are two distinct domes, forward and aft. The prominent forward dome gives me a distinct bottlenose dolphin-like appearance, and I've noticed lately at the pool that families keep wanting to get their picture swimming with me.

I also recently bought a Jeep Wrangler (second classic mid-life crisis symptom). My rationale: if I'm going to own a car, why not own one I want? Sounds like common sense, but as with many decisions in life, I'd always hesitated, frozen by an odd mix of fear and practicality.

I've found, though, that as I get older, fear and practicality have begun losing their hold on me. This is normal for men. For instance, think about how your dad or grandfather dresses. Do they appear bound by any concern for what others think of them, or for that matter by any known sense of style?

Besides, it's not like the Jeep is some flashy sports car. Its 13 years old with a four-cylinder engine. I haven't had this little horsepower under the hood since my Renault LeCar in 1987. That car was so small that when I turned on the windshield wipers the car rocked.

The Jeep, on the other hand, is big, and getting it to highway speeds requires five miles and a downhill grade. The other day on Rt. 288 a Toyota Prius passed me like I was standing still. I gave the guy a thumb's up when I passed him later – he'd driven up an embankment to stop the car, because of that whole Toyota brake thing…

I'm OK with all that – the lack of horsepower, the Twin Peaks profile, and who I am.

A younger guy down the street has a Jeep – when he drives it, hat turned backwards and shades on, he looks cool. When I drive my Jeep, I look like my grandson lent me his car while my Buick was in the shop.

Whatever. As the saying (sort of) goes: life is short (and getting shorter) – drive the Jeep first.

Retrospective Notes for *Mid-Life Catharsis*
- Well, it's seven years since this essay ran… and I still have that Jeep.
- It's impractical, loud, bumpy and the interior climate control is about what you'd expect from a tent on wheels.
- I get 12-14 miles per gallon and the car still slows into the high 40s going up a hill on the interstate, but what do

you want from a rolling air dam? A cinder block has a more aerodynamic profile and is only slightly less comfortable under your ass.

- Stacy is no more pleased with this car than she was when I first got it, and I'm not sure she's warmed to my no-hair style, either.
- And while there's no going back on my hairline, I could choose to return to a car with comfort more suiting my age.
- Nah. I think I'll enjoy life and keep the Jeep.

ONE BIG FAMILY
Originally published: December 2008

One of the great things about being a dad is that you can inculcate your kids with the illusion of infallibility right out of the gate. From the moment the child can focus on your face, you can portray yourself in stories as a hero, an intellectual giant, and a pillar of good judgment and wisdom.

So I can't figure out how it came to be that my kids' favorite story is about the time that I hit myself in the head with a baseball bat. And, believe it or not, it's actually stupider than it sounds.

When I was growing up, our family had an oversized knock-off of the classic Hippity Hop™. This fake Hippity Hop® was big and pear-shaped and sort of chemical-orange in color, and instead of a ring to hold on to (as one would find on the original Hippity Hop©), it had antlers. Not reindeer antlers but a pair of long, twisting antlers, like the horns on an Eland, curving outward from each other. We didn't know what it was called, so we just called it a Hippity Hop, but we didn't include the ™ or the ® or the ©.

Anyway, one afternoon when I was about 13 we were playing baseball in the back yard, and I got a great idea. Standing at home plate and holding my 28-inch wooden Louisville Slugger,

I asked my friend Matthew King to pitch me the Hippity Hop instead of the tennis ball we had been using.

He obliged, tossing the super-bouncy orange orb toward me in a high arcing pitch. I kept my eye on the, er, ball, as it came toward me, then unleashed a vicious tomahawk swing that I was sure would send the thing flying over the Hague's garage roof, an automatic home run.

However, the Hippity Hop knock-off and Sir Isaac Newton had a surprise in store for me, as my bat bounced back sharply off the giant rubber ball and nearly 100% of the energy of my swing was unleashed instead into the top of my forehead.

The next thing I remember, I was standing on the King's patio, leaning forward with blood pouring off my head onto the bright white concrete. My younger sister Linda was patting my back and reassuring me I'd be all right and Mrs. King was yelling for Matthew to go get my mom.

Amid all the blood and the throbbing and the chaos, one alarming question stood out clearly in my mind: why was my sister being so nice to me?

Was I dying?? I must be dying if Linda was being nice to me!!

See, my sister and I – actually, all my siblings – did not exactly get along. We didn't fight like cats and dogs... we fought more like tigers and wolves. So when Linda suddenly showed up at my side softly telling me I was OK, I was sure I was either dying or Candid Camera had staged its most violent hoax yet.

As it turns out, though, Linda was just practicing what our parents preached... and preached... and preached – that family is the most important thing a person has, and that brothers and sisters need to be there for each other, no matter what. In fact, that day was sort of a turning point for Linda and me. Over the next few years, as we moved into our teenage years, we became closer and closer – in fact, all of us did – until we became what we are now: an indivisible unit.

As we grew into adults, we also grew secure in the knowledge that no matter what happened to any one of us, the other three

ALWAYS had our back, and were supporting and encouraging each other.

It wasn't always easy. When my sister decided to move west, to Colorado and then Idaho, we knew we'd miss her, but we also knew this was what she wanted, so we supported her. Now she is very happy with her husband Lee (a Cajun forester and wildlife management professional, sort of a Daniel Boone of the Bayou) and their two beautiful kids, living, literally, in the shadow of the Grand Tetons. We couldn't be happier for her, and if the economy collapses, we'll all be moving out to live with her and survive on Lee's annual elk hunt in the High Country.

Actually, Linda may have just learned about that plan as she read this. (Yes, they are regular readers of the *Chesterfield Observer*, and in fact they have some questions about this grinding issue we seem to have here...).

Someone once asked me whether the fact that another of my siblings was buying a nice house was a problem for me. I literally did not understand the question – it was based on a zero-sum view of a family's potential happiness, as if my sibling's success was a setback for me.

I can't see how a family can operate that way and still make individual or collective progress. We may sometimes disagree, but when one of us succeeds, we all succeed, and when one of us fails, we all come together to pull the other back up to his or her feet. Simply, we are stronger together than we are apart.

Here's the thing: we just had a huge family meeting about a big decision. It took (God help us) over two years to complete and then, on Tuesday, Nov. 4, we all held a family vote, and the issue was decided.

Now it's time for our family to move forward together, to have each other's backs, so that we can ALL make progress. We will not succeed as a family (and that's what we are) and solve the big problems we ALL face if we are calling each other nasty names, undermining each other's goals, suspecting sinister motives, doubting each other's good will, or spreading rumors.

Family members do not – CANNOT – treat each other that way.

Not if we want to survive.

Retrospective Notes for *One Big Family*
- Obviously, this essay was as much about country as family.
- Unfortunately, although my siblings and I have gotten tighter, the country has gone the other direction.
- I have liberal friends who will argue until they are blue in the face that it's the Republicans' fault, and conservative friends who will argue it's the Democrats' fault, and I will tell you they are both right.
- There's lots I could say on this topic, but suffice to say that if you are sure the problems we are having are all other people's fault, then you are part of the problem. You can't change them. You can only change you. As Gandhi said, "Be the change you want to see in the world."
- That said, I'm sure you are wondering what "grinding" issue my sister Linda might have been curious about back in 2008. Long story short: after an *Observer* photographer took shots at a high school homecoming dance of kids dirty dancing, the parents of Chesterfield County lost their minds. There were news stories and letters to the editor and accusations and denunciations and for a while there I forgot all about the fact that our country had just fallen into the worst recession since 1929.
- A couple weeks later the grinding issue went away and it hasn't come up again since.
- To close the loop on the Hippity Hop, a year or so later I killed that damn thing, but it took its pound of flesh in the process. I was dragging it down the road on a 30-

foot rope tied to the back of my bike (I have no idea why), and as I went tearing down the street, the Hippity Hop skipped over toward the curb like a drunk skier and got jammed under a parked car. The good news: that thing was destroyed by the impact. The bad news: the force that destroyed it was caused by my bike going from 25 miles per hour to zero in a split second as I reached the end of my rope. Like a cartoon dog on a short leash, my bike was yanked violently backwards (and bent in half in the process). I, on the other hand, continued moving forward over my handlebars at 25 mph, at least until I hit the pavement. Head to toe, the skin on my right side was torn off in jagged patches, and the plastic of my windbreaker was shredded and embedded deep into my flesh, along with tar and rocks.

- But that son of a bitch was dead. I'm only sorry I didn't mount those orange antlers on my wall.

DAVE
Originally published: May 11, 2016

In October 1987, I had moved from Richmond, Virginia to the Caribbean to live out my life under the palm trees. I had been adrift since I graduated college two years earlier, without purpose or direction. I had figured, as long as I was adrift, why not drift on down to a sun-drenched island nearer to the Equator?

In St. Thomas, I found work and fun, but still no direction. I needed some sort of – what? maybe divine guidance? – in finding my life's direction. Dave was the unlikely messenger who delivered it.

One fateful, balmy December night, I met Dave. Well, actually, at the actual moment in question, I was drifting, asleep, on a raft of many margaritas, nearly horizontal in a white wicker chair in the corner of For the Birds, an open-air beach-side bar on the north side of St. Thomas. But someone was trying to wake me up.

This guy had apparently surveyed the dancing, drinking, partying crowd in the bar, and for a reason I never learned, chose the person passed out in the corner to be his friend.

Now he was slapping my knee, insistent: "Hey! Hey! Wake up. I need a friend. Hey, I need a friend. I just delivered a yacht from New Jersey, and I'm new to the island. Wanna be my friend?"

"Sure," I said to shut him up, and closed my eyes again.

"Let's go to Morning Star Beach tomorrow," said the tenacious drunk. "Where do you live? I'll come get you."

I gave him the address of the mouse-infested, crime-ridden, lizard-lodging fleabag hotel that was my paradise retirement home, then drifted back out to sleep on my margarita raft, knowing I'd never see the guy again.

The next morning, after a long cab ride and a brief slumber, I heard a pounding at my fleabag front door. Opening the door slowly, I squinted into the morning Caribbean sun, and beheld Dave.

By the time we arrived at his new favorite beach – which was topless, of course – Dave had told me five stories about women he'd recently met, each story wilder than the last. As we sipped beers from the cooler we'd brought and surveyed the scene, Dave explained his methods and philosophies regarding the fairer sex. But it was clear that Dave's way with women – and with everyone else in his life – was more akin to a tsunami than subtle technique. He simply swept them away.

Over the next seven months, Dave came to represent for me the personification of what living in the islands should be about. His most noticeable feature was his overwhelming personality. You didn't hang out with Dave as hung on, getting dragged along in his draft like paper behind an eighteen-wheeler.

During my time hanging on Dave on St. Thomas, I got into and out of more chaotic parties, car crashes and bar fights than I had lived through in my previous 25 years. Dave didn't just drive home the meaning of carpe diem, he wrapped it around a tree in the front yard.

Dave's next most-noticeable feature was his ceaseless drive to seduce women. He was relentless – Pepe LePew with better stuff. Pursuing women was nearly an involuntary act for him, like blinking his eyes.

And Dave was successful. Women found him enticing. His blue eyes blazed with a lust for life. His mischievous, almost devious, smile gleamed with the promise of over-the-top fun. And while he wasn't built like Adonis, Dave stood a little under six-feet tall and was in reasonably good shape, had a carefully cultivated nut-brown tan, and sported a casually tousled tangle of thick, dark hair. According to most women I met (and I met a lot through Dave), he was, all-in-all, a fairly attractive package.

The men on the island, however, weren't quite so enamored with Dave. Well, many men. Through the primal prism that men often use to judge each other, Dave was the medium-sized gorilla at the top of the tree, beating his chest, proclaiming his preeminence, challenging all comers and, not insignificantly, attracting a good number of the females. A lot of the less secure males just aren't going to like that.

Personally, I didn't give a crap. Dave's absolute, two-handed throttle-hold on life made him an overwhelming wall of fun, moving 100 miles per hour around the clock, and I was about to surf the wave.

On any given night or early morning, we could be found in one of St. Thomas' finer establishments, toasting life and convincing women to dance on the bar.

Dave was the guy who talked me into crewing on a sailboat in the Piña Colada Regatta, a local race with an optional dress code that focused on "optional." Afterwards, the seventy boats dropped anchors off a secluded beach for a party. Combine 700 men and women in equal parts, add light and dark rum and clear blue Caribbean water, and you end up with a wonderful, intoxicating mixture that I can still taste.

One early spring day, Dave decided that a group of us – three guys and two women – should take a ride on a party barge called the *Kon Tiki*. After an enjoyable, excessive morning on the boat, our group piled off the barge onto the pier, looking for entertainment. Conveniently, we found that entertainment just one pier over, at the top of a gangplank – that led onto a monstrous cruise ship.

Dave shepherded us (somehow) past the unsuspecting guard and (somehow) straight to an empty lounge, where he immediately began making drinks for, and on, the house. When the Love Boat horn sounded, we realized that the ship was getting ready to depart St. Thomas for its next port of call. It must have been a sight for the ticketed passengers to see five people running through the ship toward the gangplank, yelling that we needed to get off the damn boat.

Somehow we all made it off and back on to the pier, in search of our next stop.

We found it nearby, in the cool, white, shady confines of a pier-side establishment called Bob's Bar. Bob's regulars washed up onto the bar stools like driftwood, and tourists perched around the perimeter, gawking at the palm trees through the open-air windows that framed the establishment.

We crashed through Bob's front door like a stumbling stampede of tipsy bulls into a china shop, and immediately gravitated to a giant world map covering one wall. But to reach the map, the five of us had to stand on a row of benches – Bob's benches.

Bob protested that we were ruining his benches, staining his map and disrupting his bar. Dave called the play, and on the count of three, all five of us mooned Bob and his bar, giving the tourists something a little more interesting to gawk at.

To our genuine surprise, we were thrown out. I had been booted from bars at 2:30 in the morning before. But only with Dave have I ever been thrown out of a bar by 2:30 in the *afternoon*. We called it a day.

During my time in the islands, I found that there were two basic types of people who followed the path south to the Caribbean: those who had the guts to walk away from modern life, and those who didn't have the guts to face modern life. I had started out as the latter, but with Dave's help, I was becoming the former.

Sometimes Dave's interventions were subtle: a challenging look when I balked at talking to a woman or doing a shot. Sometimes his interventions were more direct.

I had often proclaimed that when I left St. Thomas, I was sailing off the rock, not taking a plane. Dave, for some reason, took these ridiculous declarations seriously.

As the tourist season ended and we drifted toward summer, Dave arranged a job interview for two positions crewing a 51-foot sailboat bound for the resort island of Ibiza in the Mediterranean Sea. The millionaire Dutch owner of the yacht *Jaska* liked to keep it in the Caribbean during the winter (although he rarely visited it), and then he would have it moved across the ocean to the Med so he could not sail on it there during the summer.

One balmy night we met with *Jaska*'s captain around the table in the yacht's darkened, teak wood main cabin, as she rolled gently at anchor in the Red Hook Harbor of St. Thomas. Captain Dimitri was a lean, well-muscled guy in his late twenties.

Despite some queasiness from the boat's motion (not a good omen, by the way), the interview went remarkably well – especially since my experience sailing boats matched, for example, my experience flying airliners.

"Sooo, Mr. Hansen, we need someone to help fly this Boeing 747. It will require around the clock piloting for two months, and you will have control of the airliner one-quarter of that time. Do you have any experience?"

"Uh, well, I know when to put my tray in its upright position, and I always watch the safety demonstration…"

"Terrific! You're hired! You can start by polishing that brass over there."

So, somehow, Dave had put me on a relatively small boat on an objectively huge ocean. The crew was Dave and another excellent sailor (our first mate, Ian), as well as an excellent sailor and questionable captain (Dimitri).

It was 28 years ago today, as I write this, that we set sail.

We crossed some 4,000 miles of open ocean, gliding across the surface with huge pods of dolphin, sliding down and crashing into walls of storm-driven gray waves, rolling over swells with giant whales, dodging huge tankers and freighters outside the Strait of Gibraltar, lifting beers in the Azores, Gibraltar and Ibiza with sailors from all over the world ... having the time of my life.

Yet, even as Dave and I were living this adventure together, my days surfing the Dave tidal wave were nearing their end, at least for the time being. When we reached Ibiza I would be leaving *Jaska* to head back to the States. Dave would be remaining with *Jaska* indefinitely.

I knew that, after leaving Dave's company, I would never live life so fully again. Dave is like any big wave that overtakes you: unless it tips the boat, it ultimately passes beneath and goes on without you. I knew that, even long after my compass had settled and my ocean was calm, somewhere in the world, Dave would still be raising ordinary lives to extraordinary extremes.

On separate courses then, we both grew up. I went to grad school, moved back east, met my wife Stacy, we had two kids, and they grew into strong, smart, wonderful adults. Dave stayed with *Jaska*, eventually becoming the captain, sailing around the world (several times), then becoming a yacht broker and eventually owning his own brokerage, based in Newport, Rhode Island and Ft. Lauderdale, Florida.

From time to time, Dave and I caught up. When Stacy and I went to St. Maartin for our honeymoon, we visited with Dave, who happened to be on the island. He took us out and spent a ridiculous amount of money on dinner and champagne, celebrating our marriage. Another time, my friend Darryl and I traveled to Newport for one of Dave's epic parties. And here and there, we were able to grab a beer or a meal when we happened to be in the same town.

Except for these occasional reunions, however, Dave and I were on our separate paths.

Then, three years ago, fortunately and unexpectedly, the huge wave circled the globe and came back to lift me again.

One night after looking through some old pictures of the islands, I reached out to Dave (I still have the email): "Yo dude, thinking about you. When can we catch up in real life? When will you be back in the mid-Atlantic? Or maybe I can figure out a way to catch up with you in your travels. Let me know. – Chuck"

Dave wrote back almost immediately. He had an idea, something that was very important to him, and he had been thinking about me as a writer who could help out. Was I interested?

Was I interested?? Absolutely.

Over these last three years, Dave and I and Sean (a friend of Dave's and now a friend of mine) spent hundreds of hours and thousands of emails and conversations putting the project together.

Dave was doing it again, challenging me to seize the day. He was determined to see this project through, and attacked it with every bit of his typical energy, and drove us to do the same.

Dave was still that tidal wave that accelerated the lives of everyone around him... until last week, when Dave died unexpectedly.

I could never imagine a life force like Dave not being alive. But I also could never imagine Dave ever being old. So I guess I was not shocked when I got the call.

Not shocked, but terribly sad. Apart from Stacy and our kids and members of my family, Dave probably had the greatest positive impact on my life, helping me permanently change my outlook. I had explored the tropics, drank rum and danced on the bar. I had awakened from my slumber, with the help of my buddy Dave. And I carried his philosophy of carpe diem with me, from that first day on Morningstar Beach through our work together on his project, 29 years later.

Now, with Dave's death, the project has probably died with him. But it's not a loss, at least not to me. All I wanted was to help my friend Dave get this thing launched. And although that probably won't happen now, it was a gift to get the chance reconnect so closely with Dave over the past few years.

Either way, whether during the years that we were mostly out of touch or when we were together again working on his project, Dave was always with me. As I navigated life, built a marriage with Stacy and we raised our family, grappled with work and the future, Dave always was my crew mate… goading me, encouraging me, challenging me, slapping my knee and waking me up, to remind me: *Seize the day*!

And he still is.

Thank you, Dave. I am going to miss you.

Retrospective Notes for *Dave*
- I "wrote" this essay in May 2016, after hearing about Dave's death.
- In fact, however, I actually wrote much of it years before, as part of a never-published book about my time in the Virgin Islands and crossing the Atlantic on *Jaska* with Dave.
- I think one day I will publish this book. Maybe not. We'll see.
- But every day I will think about Dave and how he changed my life.

KEEP ME IN, COACH!
Originally published: July 2011

Health experts tell us that once we hit 40 and our metabolism slows, we should get more exercise. Based on that advice, I guess I need to quit softball, since I get more exercise walking from my car to the field than I do during the game.

I play in a C-level church league on a team made up of old men and a couple of whippersnappers under 35. At 48, I am not the senior team member, but I play older thanks to my exercise regimen of getting up every morning and lying down every night. I'll put it this way: My Wii-Fit age is 9-1-1.

No worries though. Slow-pitch softball has all the excitement of other sports but, at C-level anyway, much of the danger is reduced by the laws of physics. For example, the other night I nearly collided with another big man on my team. We all know that Force = Mass x Acceleration. However, in this case, while there was considerable total mass involved, the force of the potential collision was very low since acceleration was nearly nonexistent.

Another example: I have scars all over my right leg from years of sliding into bases, but none of the scars are new. These days I can't get up enough speed to accomplish a slide. Try as I might, now I just sort of slowly topple over near the base.

Still, we try hard, and it can be difficult sometimes to reconcile the intense competition with the fact that it is a church league, and there is a group prayer at the game's end. Still, at the end of a hard-fought game, heart still pumping and adrenaline surging, the prayer can be as meaningful as a Sunday service.

Another positive is that often we are playing as the sun is setting. Between pitches, there is plenty of time to admire God's handiwork as the clouds go from white to red and orange to blue. Watching the light of the sun vivifying these clouds, I think about Ralph Waldo Emerson's take on divinity: "Our soul descends into us from we know not where." Emerson also said, "Man is a stream whose source is unseen."

Clouds are clouds are clouds. It is the sun's light that animates them, that brings to life their whites, reds, oranges, blues and even silver linings – depending on the angle of the sun relative to the clouds. And when the sun is gone, a cloud is nearly invisible – the body of the cloud remains, but the animating force is absent.

The difference between clouds and people is that we choose our position relative to the light that animates us. We can put ourselves in a position to create the reds or the oranges or the whites or the silver linings, or we can hide from the light and remain dark.

We also can choose to take that energy that comes to us, from we know not where, and channel it into celebrating life, by spending time with family and friends, doing good and meaningful work, helping others – or even playing softball poorly.

Retrospective Notes for *Keep Me In, Coach!*
- One of my favorites.

ABOUT THE AUTHOR

Chuck Hansen is an award-winning author and humorist. In addition to his books, Chuck's writing has appeared in publications in Virginia and across the country. Chuck also speaks frequently, bringing his unique, thoughtful humor to business and association conferences and community group meetings.

Before finding his direction, Chuck drifted through many jobs, including copier salesman, blackjack dealer, telemarketer, daycare teacher, private detective, donut maker, bouncer in a Caribbean saloon and crew on a 51-foot sailboat crossing the North Atlantic.

While on that boat, Chuck took the helm in his life, going on to earn a master's degree and serve as press secretary for a member of Congress, speechwriter for a Virginia governor, and executive speechwriter and communications practitioner with five Fortune 500 companies.

Chuck and his wife Stacy have two adult children (Daniel and Madison) and live in beautiful Midlothian, Virginia.

For more information, to get on Chuck's mailing list, or to contact Chuck, visit his website at chuckhansen.com.

www.ingramcontent.com/pod-product-compliance
Lightning Source LLC
Chambersburg PA
CBHW060158050426
42446CB00013B/2890